BOOK PLAY

BOOK PLAY

Creative Adventures in Handmade Books

Margaret Couch Cogswell

LARK
CRAFTS

Asheville

LARK CRAFTS

An Imprint of Sterling Publishing
387 Park Avenue South
New York, NY 10016

ISBN 978-1-4547-0396-9

Library of Congress Cataloging-in-Publication Data

Cogswell, Margaret Couch, 1959-
   Book play / Margaret Couch Cogswell. -- First Edition.
      pages cm
   Includes index.
   ISBN 978-1-4547-0396-9
   1. Book design--Handbooks, manuals, etc. 2. Artists' books. I. Title.
   Z246.C38 2013
   002--dc23

                                    2012020871

Distributed in Canada by Sterling Publishing
c/o Canadian Manda Group, 165 Dufferin Street
Toronto, Ontario, Canada M6K 3H6
Distributed in the United Kingdom by GMC Distribution Services
Castle Place, 166 High Street, Lewes, East Sussex, England BN7 1XU
Distributed in Australia by Capricorn Link (Australia) Pty. Ltd.
P.O. Box 704, Windsor, NSW 2756, Australia

For information about custom editions, special sales, and premium and
corporate purchases, please contact Sterling Special Sales at 800-805-5489
or specialsales@sterlingpublishing.com.

Email academic@larkbooks.com for information about desk and examination copies.
The complete policy can be found at larkcrafts.com.

Manufactured in China

2 4 6 8 10 9 7 5 3 1

larkcrafts.com

THE BASICS

the Projects →

Bookbinding and Bookmaking 12
  Paper 12
  Basic Bookmaking Tool Kit 13
  Safety 13
  Tools and Materials 14
  The Anatomy of a Book 15
  Folding Paper 20
  Cutting Paper and Book Board 21
  Making a Book Cover 22
  Binding 23

Creative Techniques 28
  Drawing and Journaling 28
  Painting 31
  Collage 33
  Sewing 35

Working with Papier-Mâché, Tin, and Wire 38
  Papier-Mâché 38
  Tin 40
  Wire 43

Artist Features
  Gwen Diehn 54
  Doug Beube 70
  Frank Brannon 84
  Jim Cogswell 127
  Heather Allen-Hietala 131
  Dolph Smith 140

Resources 143
Acknowledgments 143
About the Author 143
Index 144

CONVENTIONAL BOOKS

Book Card.....46

Small Accordion
Storybook with Cloth Bag.....50

Zippity-Do-Da Book.....72

Book-Board Covers.....75

Travel Companion.....80

Unbound Book.....100

Digestives.....103

Bottle Cap Accordion.....106

Word Play.....124

Pencil Birds.....128

The Dispenser.....132

Air Mail.....134

Matchbox Book 56

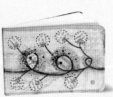

Repurposed
Surface Notebooks 60

Cloth Books 64

Pocket Book 86

Margaret's Journal 90

Travel Journal 94

Wheelie Bird 110

Head Case 115

Storyboard on Wheels 120

Book Ball 137

UN-CONVENTIONAL BOOKS

INTRODUCTION

When I was little, I was such a slow reader that books were often my last choice in a list of pastimes. I loved listening to my mother read stories, and books filled the walls of our house, but the craft table and the yard outside were bigger draws. If given the choice, I always picked movement over sitting still.

Books were, and still are, objects to me. As a child I was more interested in turning the pages, looking at the illustrations and the configuration of letters on the page than what was actually written there. I often imagined what I thought the text or images were referencing—they were a spark to ignite my own stories.

As I grew up, I learned to enjoy reading the stories that are contained within books. Even so, to this day when I read a book I must tell myself to sit still and be patient when I see a page full of words. It takes discipline to learn this because I'm used to learning through doing, but it's worth it.

The idea that a book is an exciting three-dimensional object is what led me to create my own books and to push the concept of what defines a book. It's an intuitive process for me, but the outcome usually renders a "book" that includes physical action, a story, and a spark for the viewer's imagination—plus a little humor thrown in for good measure, because I believe generating a smile or laugh is a worthwhile goal. Humor brings people to the table, and then you can feed them something a bit more serious. I've come to think of myself more as a storyteller than a book artist. I try to keep things fresh and to approach materials and ideas in a direct way, much as a child does—a playful approach executed by an adult hand.

I hope you will find this book to be a spark for your own imagination, as visually interesting as it is informative. I'll start with thoughts on basic tools and materials in my own studio and move on to basic techniques. From there I've tried to provide a group of conventional and unconventional projects that will be a jumping-off point for your own "book play." To round out and fill in my gaps, I've invited six creative people to share their thoughts on a range of topics related to books and creativity.

Thanks for joining me here between the pages.

Margaret

THE
BASICS

BOOKMAKING AND BOOKBINDING

PAPER

The varieties of paper used when making books are endless. Considering the purpose of the book is the most important criterion for me. When I first started making books I experimented with many different papers, often without regard to its grain or standard purpose. Having choices and using paper unconventionally were more important to me—I'm a bit oppositional, and following rules is hard. Over time I have narrowed my choices somewhat. Through experimentation I have learned which papers I can depend on.

Different papers offer different qualities, and some of the best papers offer a range of qualities, thereby allowing for flexibility. Good paper is like a good friend: dependable, flexible, and honest. Having said that, I'm still open to using other paper besides one of my favorites if the project calls for it. I want all the materials I use, not only the paper, to make sense within the context of the piece. Everything needs to work and support the overall message or theme. These considerations give depth to a piece, which in turn adds richness and internal structure. These sound like intellectual decisions on my part, and they are to a certain degree, but in real time they are intuitive choices. My head is following along while my gut is guiding the way. "Trust your gut" is my number-one rule.

Most of the paper I use in my work is commercial (not handmade), and it's often recycled or repurposed paper. In my studio, paper falls into two major categories: decorative and nondecorative.

DECORATIVE PAPER

I have a flat file filled with decorative paper. It's a collection that I have gathered over time. If I like it and I can afford it, I buy it. This collection provides me with a range of available options when I'm working on a project. It also feeds the collage bin. Small, leftover pieces end up on my studio table in a container that I use as source material for collage. I buy several sheets of my favorite papers, but usually one sheet of any given paper will suffice for most projects. I try to get a range of weights, from midweight to tissue weight. From time to time I visit a paper store and buy new designs and some old favorites to keep myself stocked with different choices. For me, going to a paper store is as good as going to a candy store. It's very exciting!

I also have a supply of paste paper (a type of handpainted paper) and marbled paper that I have made, as well as any found paper that appeals to me. If something catches my eye, it's usually worth having it around. Our instincts draw us to certain colors and shapes sometimes before we even know how they will fit into the bigger picture.

NONDECORATIVE PAPER

This category includes plain text paper for the inside of books, paper used for covers, used books that I deconstruct for the pages, and various other plain papers. There are three papers I use for most projects.

Hahnemühle Ingres or Fabriano: Light- to midweight, high-quality paper that comes in a range of colors; good for text paper and end sheets. Can handle collage and light watercolor or gouache. Acid-free.

Rives BFK: Heavyweight, high-quality paper that comes in a few colors; good for text paper, drawings, collage, and cards. Can handle paint, collage, and watercolor or gouache. Acid-free.

Murano: Midweight textured paper that comes in a wide range of colors; economical; good for text paper, scrapbook or photo album paper, and collage with low moisture. Acid-free.

Papermaking is an art form in itself. There are many good books and resources in bookstores and on the Web. The best way to learn about paper is to buy a sheet or two of different kinds and experiment.

You'll quickly notice that you have a natural affinity for some types.

There are two qualities of both commercial and handmade paper you want to be aware of: acidity and grain. Acid-free paper is paper that has a neutral pH and is archival (can be preserved for a long time). Most of the text papers I use are acid-free, but I'm not a stickler about it. I take into account what I am making and the purpose for the book when deciding whether all the materials I use need to be acid-free. If a paper is acid-free, it says so in the product description.

The grain of paper refers to the direction of the fibers that make up the paper. You need to determine the grain of any paper for certain situations. When paper gets wet, the fibers swell, and then they shrink as it dries. This can cause the paper to curl, buckle, or wrinkle. In bookbinding there are different ways to compensate or counteract this natural response. I will address this in the section on adhesives (page 19).

Handmade paper doesn't have a specific grain because the fibers are going in all directions. This occurs during the papermaking process. Commercial papers do have a grain, and there are several ways to determine the direction. My preferred way is to cut a square of the paper and, with my eyes closed (this helps me concentrate on the feel rather than the visual), hold the square in front of me. I gently bend it in one direction and then the other, as if I were going to fold it in half. You can feel that the paper bends more easily one way than the other. The direction with less resistance is the direction of the grain.

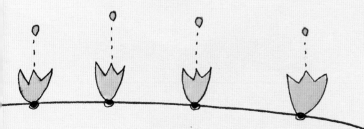

BASIC BOOKMAKING TOOL KIT

In the following sections, I will discuss some of my favorite tools for bookmaking as well as for various creative techniques, but here are the basics you should have on hand for just about every project in this book:

Bone folder (page 16)

Book glue (page 19)

Craft knife (page 14)

Mars plastic eraser

Fettling knife (page 14)

Glue brush for applying book glue

Glue stick

Pencil

Needle tool (page 16)

Metal ruler

Scissors (page 16)

Self-healing mat (page 16)

Utility knife (page 16)

SAFETY

Most of the materials used in these projects are nontoxic, but occasionally there are safety concerns. Common sense and responsible studio practices cover most of the bases. Here are a few of the essentials:

– Always use a mask when sanding, especially when sanding milk paint.

– Keep food containers and studio supply containers separate.

– Wear gloves (page 41) when working with tin or other metals.

– Ensure proper ventilation when using spray paint, shellac, and fixatives.

TOOLS AND MATERIALS

Today's bookbinders are lucky: now more than ever, bookbinding tools and materials are widely available online, through bookbinding suppliers, and from arts and crafts stores. There is a tool for almost every task. But since my techniques are usually simple, my tools tend to be, too.

TOOLS

Corner rounder: This works like a hole punch, but it enables you to round the corners of paper—a very appealing detail on text paper as well as covers. These tools come in several styles. The nicer ones enable you to cut large numbers of pages at a time, and even book board if they're industrial strength. Rounded corners are a small detail with a big impact on overall appeal. You can find simple versions at craft supply stores. For a more substantial one, check online bookbinding suppliers (see page 143).

Craft knife: Although I prefer to use a utility knife for most of my cutting because the handle is fatter (it's easier for me to hold), a utility knife in not an ideal tool for making delicate cuts. When making books I tend to go back and forth between my utility knife and a craft knife with retractable, snap-off blades.

Fettling knife: 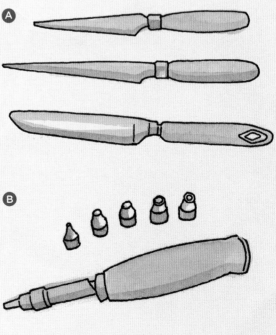 This is actually a tool for potters, but I love it. It looks like a tapered knife with one edge rounded and the other thin and flat. It's not expensive and has a range of uses in the book studio. Potters use it for cutting clay, but I use it for tearing and scoring paper. In a pinch it can double as a screwdriver and makes a most excellent letter opener!

Japanese hole punch with 1, 2, 3, and 4 mm tips: Ⓑ This is an ingenious tool and well worth the money. Essentially, it's a spring-loaded drill that has inter-changeable tips for making holes of different diameters in paper, leather, and thin board. It cuts holes easily and cleanly without leaving any type of burr or ragged edge. It's hard to achieve this repetition with any other tool. You can buy the handle/drill and tips separately or as a set. There are a few different ones out there, but don't skimp because this is a tool that will last a lifetime, and the cheaper ones tend not to be as smooth in their drill action.

Because the tip will cut past the paper and partially into whatever is beneath it, when using this hole punch, I keep a small self-healing mat about 4 x 6 inches (10 x 15.2 cm) to use as a hard surface under any paper as I'm punching. When my large self-healing mats get old, I cut

Anatomy of a Book

A book is made up of multiple parts and each of these parts has a name. The cover consists of the front board, back board, and spine. The top of the book is the head, and the bottom of the book is the tail. The side opposite the spine is the fore edge. The inside of the book contains the text block. The text block consists of a group of signatures (see page 23), which are folded sheets that form pages. Take a moment to familiarize yourself with these terms!

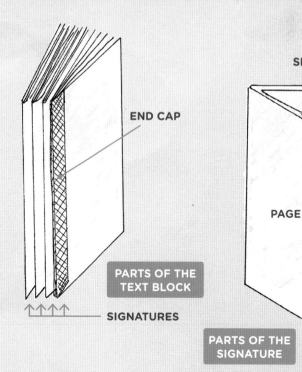

hair shirt

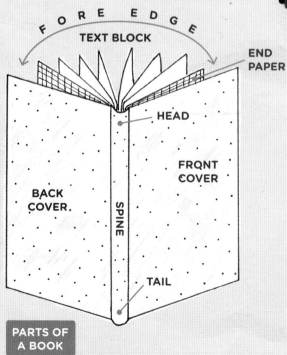

FORE EDGE

TEXT BLOCK

END PAPER

HEAD

FRONT COVER

BACK COVER.

SPINE

TAIL

PARTS OF A BOOK

END CAP

SHEET

PAGE

PARTS OF THE TEXT BLOCK

SIGNATURES

PARTS OF THE SIGNATURE

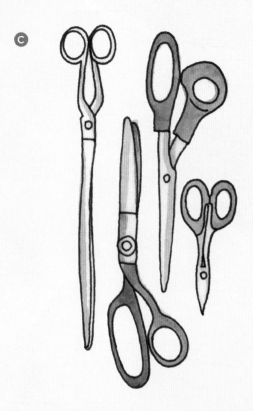

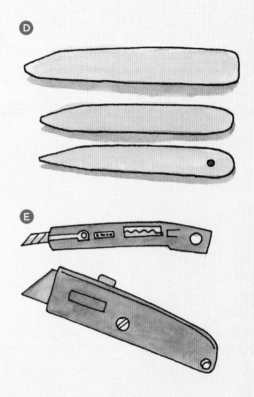

them into smaller pieces to use for just this purpose. If you don't have an old mat, a scrap of book board or Davey board (page 17) works well, too.

Needles: You can purchase needles specifically for bookbinding, but I use cotton darning needles because I can buy them at my local sewing store; my favorite sizes are 6 and 7. Darners are long needles with long eyes and are typically used for basting cotton. I use both straight and bent needles, depending on the binding.

Needle tool: Like the fettling knife, this is also a clay tool. Sometimes called a pin tool, it is a thick, straight pin on the end of a wooden handle—essentially an awl that isn't tapered. I like this tool because it has a straight pin, is lightweight, and is a good price. When I'm binding a cloth book I use three to five of these at a time to make the holes for binding, so I keep a number on hand. You can use an awl, if necessary, instead.

Scissors: Cutting paper dulls scissors, so I have one pair of scissors for fabric and one pair for paper. It's important to have a quality pair to use for collage and for other stages of the bookmaking process.

Self-healing mats: I recommend buying one of these that measures at least 18 x 24 inches (45.7 x 61 cm), with gridded measurements. If you plan on using a Japanese hole punch (see page 14), I also recommend buying a smaller one, about 4 x 6 inches (10 x 15.2 cm).

Teflon bone folder: A whole section could be devoted to bone folders. They are such an essential tool to anyone working with books and paper. They come in many shapes and sizes that correspond to different tasks, but most of us only need one or two bone folders to cover the range of our projects. I own three but really only use one. The perfect bone folder for you is definitely a personal choice based on how it feels in your hand and what you need it to do. While traditional bone folders are (obviously) made of bone, I prefer ones made from Teflon. The Teflon keeps glue, paint, pencil, or anything else from sticking to it and won't leave a shine on book cloth. Mine is a bit heavier and thicker, with one tapered, pointed end and the other tapered flat.

Utility knife: This knife is good for hand-cutting book board and other heavy or thick materials. I use one with a replaceable, retractable blade. Change the blade as soon as it gets dull to prevent ragged edges when cutting.

MATERIALS

Book board: Book board is also known as Davey board and binder's board; you'll hear all three names to describe this heavy board used for covers in bookbinding. It generally comes in three thicknesses, measured in millimeters or points (pt): 1.7 mm (68 pt), 1.9 mm (74 pt), and 2.1 mm (80 pt). (A point is a measure of thousandths of an inch; 80 points equals 80/1,000 inch.) The general rule is the larger the book, the heavier the board used. For me it's an aesthetic decision made with the project in mind. You can find it at art supply stores. Whenever I buy board I always mark the grain direction on the board by drawing pencil lines in the direction of the grain 2 to 3 inches (5 to 7.5 cm) apart. This way no matter how you cut the board you still have grain lines on what's left. Note that I stay away from using mat board for book covers because it warps.

Homemade book board: When I want a very thin board or just want to save a few dollars, I make my own from shirt board or cereal boxes. The thin, gray board that comes as stiffener or backing when you buy certain clothes or linens makes great book board for small projects. Flattened cereal boxes headed for the recycling bin also make good board after the shiny side is given a quick brush with some 150-grit sandpaper. If a thicker board is needed, these thin boards can be laminated (glued) together to create any thickness you want. I like to use three layers of shirt board when making my Book Card (page 46) and Small Accordion Storybook (page 50).

To use these for a project, you must first laminate them. Find the direction of the grain and mark it on the board with pencil. Brush book glue (page 19) on one side of the board and, matching the grain, glue it to another board. Continue until the desired thickness of board is reached. Put under a weight (see page 18) for at least two hours.

Book cloth: Book cloth is fabric that has a thin paper backing so it can be attached without moisture and glue seeping through the fabric. It is traditionally used to cover book board, but it has many uses in bookmaking. It comes in a variety of colors and styles, but sometimes I want something a bit more fun. That's when I make my

own book cloth. There are a couple of ways to do this. One uses a product called Sulky Fuse 'n Stitch found at fabric stores. It's a fusible paper that you iron onto the back of your fabric. The other way is to brush a thin layer of book glue on thin paper and adhere it to the back side of your fabric; use a bone folder to smooth out air bubbles. I have found that thin copier paper works well unless you need something larger. You do have to be careful not to use an excess amount of glue, or it will seep through to the front of the fabric; do a test piece first.

End caps: End caps are decorative wraps across the spine edge of signatures—other than the first and last signatures—between the end sheets. End caps are usually found in exposed spine bindings such as the Coptic (page 26) and stab (page 25). Their measurements vary, but mine are usually 2 inches (5 cm) wide by the height of the book. When folded in half lengthwise, they become 1-inch (2.5 cm) caps. See the Cloth Books (page 64) or Travel Journal (page 94) for an example of end caps.

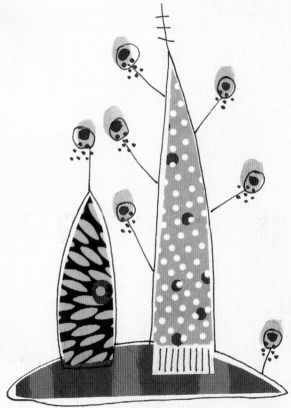

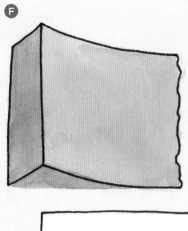

End sheets: End sheets are decorative paper at the beginning and end of the book. They are an opportunity to bring in additional color to the text block and are usually the same or lighter weight than the text paper. They can either be the sheet size or page size plus 1½ inches (3.8 cm) on the spine edge. **F**

Linen thread: This thread can be purchased in 3-ply or 4-ply, and waxed or unwaxed. It's even available in a large range of colors. You can find it at bookbinding and basket making suppliers, in some craft stores, and online. The 4-ply waxed thread, which has a heavy coat of wax, is more common, but I prefer 3-ply unwaxed because I find the thinner thread easier to bind and I prefer to wax it myself with a beeswax disk. I keep a good selection of colors in my studio so I'll have options when I'm working on a project.

Weights: When making books, there are many steps when parts or the whole need to be placed under a weight to prevent warping. You can buy a book press or make one of your own. I have the simple, homemade version: four clean 12 x 18-inch (30.5 x 45.7 cm) medium-density fiberboard (MDF) pieces with two sheets of waxed paper in between each piece of MDF (which means six sheets of waxed paper will be needed for four boards) and old-fashioned flat irons on top for weight. **G** In a pinch, a stack of hardcover books on a flat surface works just as well. Always remember to put waxed paper or freezer paper between two layers of board. This separates the moisture from the MDF and keeps any excess glue from creating a bond between it and your work.

ADHESIVES

Book glues: Just as with paper, everyone who works with books has different preferences for adhesives. I primarily use polyvinyl acetate (PVA), also known as white glue or school glue. It's a water-based, nontoxic glue that is very versatile. For most projects I mix a combination of PVA and methylcellulose that I call book glue.

Methylcellulose comes in powder form that you mix with water. Added to PVA, it extends the glue and lengthens the drying time. This is helpful when you are brushing glue onto a book cover and need to allow more time for placing the cover. Although I can buy prepared versions of these combinations, it's easier and cheaper to mix them myself. I store these mixtures in new airtight containers. For the longest shelf life, the containers should be new or never had food stored in them. That way, there is no chance for lingering bacteria to spoil your mixture. Both PVA and methylcellulose have a long shelf life, but they don't like to be frozen. With all the glues I list, be sure to read the manufacturers' directions.

Here are the combinations I use most in my studio:

Book glue: two parts PVA to one part methylcellulose. I use this glue for all basic gluing tasks in bookmaking.

Thinner book glue: one part PVA to one part methylcellulose. I use this combination whenever thinner glue is helpful, as in the Repurposed Surface Notebook (page 60).

Straight PVA: I use this only when I need a thicker, faster-acting glue for paper.

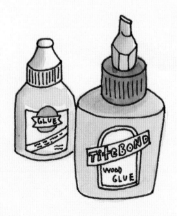

Glue sticks: I love a good glue stick. My favorite is UHU Stic colored glue stick. It rubs on purple, so you can tell exactly where the glue is. Once the glue dries, the color disappears. Very handy! It's nontoxic and archival. As far as I'm concerned, the best quality of glue sticks is that they are a "dry" glue. This means you don't have to worry about moisture and warping like you do with "wet" glue (like book glue). UHU Stic adhesion is very strong and doesn't yellow over time. I use a glue stick for all of my collages. Note: Glue sticks work best when you only twist a small amount up at a time; you have much more control this way. Also, remember to keep the cap on the stick when not using it, or when there are gaps of time while you are working. It will stay fresher and smoother so much longer. (As you can tell, I'm quite picky about my glue stick.)

Wood glue: This is in the PVA family, but it has an additional ingredient to help with slippage. It is often referred to as "yellow glue." I use this when gluing wood (obvious, I know).

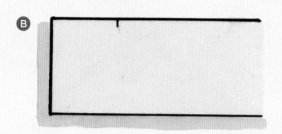

FOLDING PAPER

To fold paper, line up the top two corners of the paper on a flat, smooth surface. With your middle and index fingers pinning the top corners down gently, smooth the paper along the top toward the fold with your other hand. Continue to keep your fingers holding down the corners as you press the rest of the fold. Run a bone folder along the fold to set the fold. Ⓐ

ACCORDION FOLD

To create a consistent accordion fold, attention to detail is required. Cut or tear a strip of paper the desired length. Working from left to right on a smooth, flat surface, hold the left-hand side of the paper along the left-hand side of a ruler. Find the page width and gently make a small fold (or a light pencil mark) on the top edge of the paper to the right. Ⓑ Remove the ruler. Fold the paper to the left (back toward the end) at the point of the small fold you just made. Ⓒ Be sure to keep the top and bottom edges lined up. I know my fold is aligned when I can't see the lower layer of paper. Set the fold with a bone folder. Holding the fold you just created, Ⓓ fold the paper that is now extending out to the left back to the right at the exact edge of your starting point. Smooth out that fold, again being sure to align the top and bottom edges of the paper. Set the fold with a bone folder. Keep repeating this process until you reach the end of your strip. Ⓔ

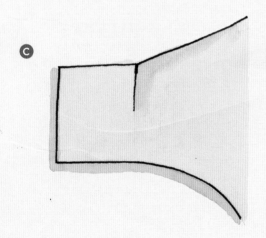

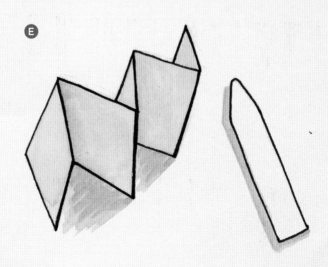

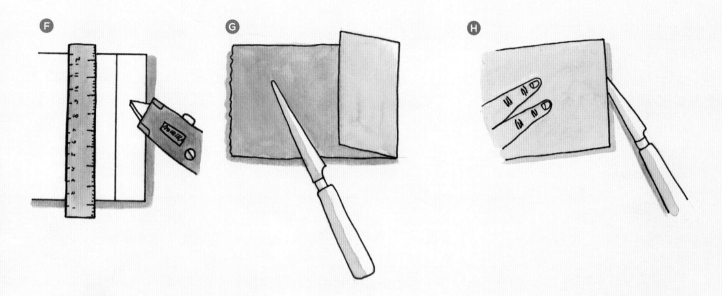

CUTTING PAPER AND BOOK BOARD

A sharp craft knife blade, self-healing cutting mat, and metal ruler are keys to the most effective and efficient way to cut paper. Line up the paper on your cutting mat. Line the ruler up with the desired cutting line. Placing even pressure on the ruler, draw your craft-knife blade down the ruler to make the cut. If the paper is thick you might need to draw the knife down a couple of times. It's easier and safer to make several light cuts than to try and cut through with only one pass.

Cutting book board is the same as cutting paper except for the fact that board is so much thicker. Because the board is hard to cut, I usually use a more substantial utility knife with a fresh blade instead of a craft knife. It will definitely take more than one pass down the ruler to cut through board. F

I always stand up when cutting paper or board so that I can easily see what I am doing. A standing position also allows for better control of the ruler and knife.

Tearing paper is another option. The key to tearing paper smoothly is to make sure the fold is set. Running a bone folder along the fold front and back is good practice. There are several ways to tear paper once the fold is set. One method is to use a metal tear bar that you put on top of your paper at the fold line, hold the bar steady, and pull the paper upward against the sharp edge of the bar. Tear bars look like rulers without the numbers, and one edge is tapered and sharp. Another method is to fold your paper back and forth a couple of times. Open the paper up and use one hand to hold one side flat alongside the fold while the other hand pulls from the other side. My method of choice is to use a fettling knife (page 14). G An old butter knife makes an adequate stand-in if you don't have a fettling knife. Put the fettling knife into the fold at the bottom of the paper. The knife should be held at a 90° angle. Hold the paper down with your other hand. Using an upward, steady sawing motion, run the knife up the fold. H

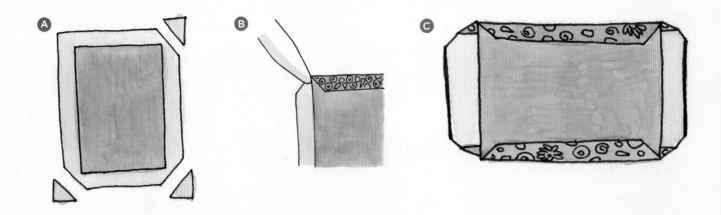

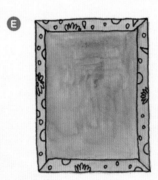

MAKING A BOOK COVER

Many of the conventional book projects in this book have covers made from book board wrapped with paper or fabric. We'll tackle the basics here, and special attention to the corners will make for a tidy and smooth cover.

Start by brushing book glue onto one board. Then center the glued side of the board down onto the back of your cover paper. There should be ¼ inch (6 mm) of the paper extending past the board all around. Use your bone folder to smooth out any air bubbles.

Trim all four corners of the paper to ⅛ inch (3 mm) of each board corner. ⒜ Working on the back, brush glue onto the vertical sides of the paper extending past the board. Fold the edges of the paper over the board. Use your bone folder to smooth out any air bubbles.

Using the tip of your bone folder, tuck the corners toward the unglued sides of the paper. ⒝ ⒞

Brush glue onto the two remaining sides of paper. Fold the edges of the paper over the board. ⒟ Use your bone folder to smooth out any air bubbles. ⒠

Repeat the process for the second board. Put both boards under a weight.

BINDING

It's true that the binding process involves multiple steps. But don't be intimidated when you read the words "Coptic" or "seven-hole pamphlet stitch." With patience and a little practice, you'll be binding books before you know it.

CREATING SIGNATURES

The pages of a book are typically organized into groups that are folded and nested. These bundles, known as signatures, make it so paper can easily and efficiently be sewn onto the spine. The number of pages in a signature varies, as does the number of signatures, depending on the weight of the paper and the purpose and style of your book. Groups of signatures make up the text block of the book (see page 15).

F

MAKING A TEMPLATE

The first step in binding is to make a template. A template allows you to punch multiple holes in your signatures and cover accurately, quickly, and consistently. The holes are also known as sewing stations.

To make the template, cut a piece of midweight scrap paper 4 inches (10 cm) wide by the exact height of your book. Fold it in half vertically. With a ruler, measure 1/2 inch (1.3 cm) from the top and bottom and mark on the center fold. Unfold the paper template. Fold it in half horizontally. Unfold the paper again and mark where the two folds (horizontal and vertical) intersect: you now have a three-hole template.

It's easy to expand the template to five and seven holes. With the paper unfolded, after folding it in half horizontally to make the center mark, fold it in half again, matching the horizontal center with each 1/2-inch (1.3 cm) mark. Mark these new folds with a pencil. This gives you five evenly spaced holes without measuring. For seven holes, fold it in half one more time before matching the horizontal center and marking the folds.

Lay the first signature in an open phone book and put the template on top inside the fold, aligning it carefully with the top of the signature. Punch the sewing stations with a needle tool or an awl. **F** Repeat with the remaining signatures. If you have more than one signature, be sure to maintain their order before you begin to sew them together. Follow the same steps to punch the sewing stations in the cover.

THREE-HOLE PAMPHLET STITCH

This simple structure is used for smaller books, usually no taller than 6 inches (15.2 cm), with a small number of pages. Punch the holes marked on the template— approximately ½ inch (1.3 cm) from the head and tail of the book and another halfway between them in both the text block and the cover.

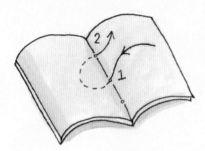

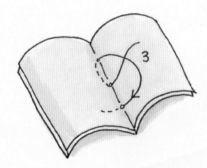

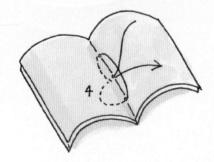

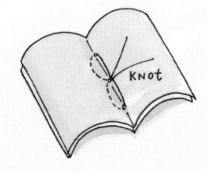

To complete the most basic pamphlet stitch, cut a piece of thread that is two times the height of the book plus a few extra inches, and thread a needle. Do not tie a knot at the end of the thread, but leave enough thread at the end for a square knot. Begin to sew at the desired knot location. Traditionally, you begin in the center sewing station so the knot is hidden on the inside. Open the book to the center spread, and follow the diagram at left. **A**

To make a square knot, cross the right end over the left end (which forms a half knot). Next, cross the left over the right end: this forms a square knot. **B** Pull tight and clip each end to ¼ inch (6 mm).

Because the paper has thickness, there will be a bit of creep on the fore edge, meaning the outside pages of the signature will not jut out as far as the inside ones. You can trim these pages if you want a sharp, clean edge. Using a metal ruler and a self-healing cutting mat, line the ruler up square with the top of the text block, holding the cover out of the way. If the book is thick, clamp the ruler to the table or to a board beneath the book to keep it from slipping. Use a very sharp craft knife and hold it vertically to keep the edges of the pages aligned. Draw it along the ruler, using fairly light pressure so that the knife is cutting the paper, not shredding it. Repeat until you have cut cleanly through all the sheets.

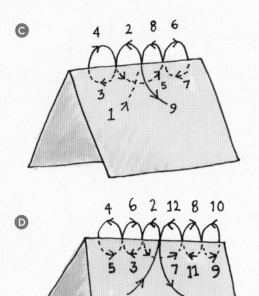

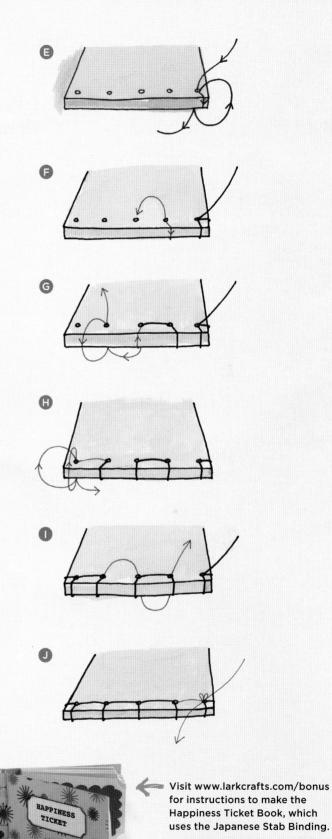

FIVE- OR SEVEN-HOLE PAMPHLET STITCH

If the book is taller, you'll want to add more sewing stations to strengthen its structure. A basic guideline is to leave 1½ to 2 inches (3.8 to 5.1 cm) between the three middle holes (for a five-hole pamphlet) and between the five middle holes (for a seven-hole pamphlet).

For the five-hole book, follow the diagram at. C For the seven-hole book D, the sewing pattern is the same, except that you add a stitch on either side as you sew. You can also begin either of these structures on the outside if you want your knot and tassel to show as part of your design.

JAPANESE STAB BINDING

This is a good method for binding a number of single-sided sheets—collections of one-sided drawings, blank sheets for a photo album, or other items—although, as a disadvantage, it does not open flat. The stitching pattern for this book is much simpler than it looks and can be adapted for any number of holes. Follow E through J.

Visit www.larkcrafts.com/bonus for instructions to make the Happiness Ticket Book, which uses the Japanese Stab Binding.

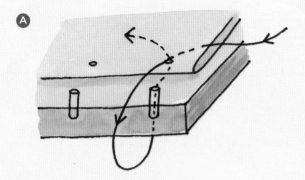

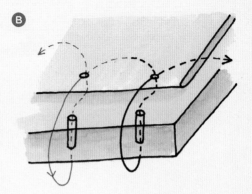

SINGLE-NEEDLE COPTIC STITCH

This style of binding creates a flexible book that's ideal for journals and sketchbooks because it opens flat, allowing you to easily write, draw, and paint on its pages. I've used it for Margaret's Journal (page 90) and the Travel Journal (page 94).

With the spine facing you, place the last signature of the book on the back cover, again with the spine facing you. Beginning at station one inside the signature, bring the needle to the outside and then up through the first hole in the cover. Ⓐ Leave a tail about 3 inches (7.6 cm) long inside the signature. Go back into the first signature—pulling the threads snugly but being careful not to tear the paper—and move to the second station, repeating the step. Ⓑ Continue to work your way across the spine, going down through each station and then back up again. Ⓒ

When you have come out of station four, add another signature and come up inside the fourth station on that signature. Ⓓ Work your way back to the opposite end of the book, attaching this second signature. As you come down out of the end stations at the head and tail of the book, make a kettle stitch by slipping the needle under the connecting stitch between the first signature and the cover, bringing it again to the outside,

and then going back into the station in the next signature. Ⓔ For the second and third stations, make a chain stitch Ⓕ by making a loop under the stitch from the previous row, and then going back into the hole you just exited. Ⓖ

When you get back to the first station, secure the tail you left at the beginning by going up through the first hole of the first signature and tying a square knot (page 24, figure B). Then come back out of this signature. Make a kettle stitch. Add the third signature to the book; bring the needle up into the first station in this signature. Ⓗ Repeat this stitch pattern, working up and down the spine of the book and adding signatures as you get to each end.

Attach the cover and the last signature at the same time by repeating the process you used at the beginning: come out of each station, make a kettle stitch with the signature below, and then attach the cover by going through the holes in the cover. When you have sewn through all the stations, bring the thread back to the inside of the last signature and tie a pair of slipknots Ⓘ under the last running stitch in the center of this signature. Ⓙ Trim the threads to about ½ inch (1.3 cm).

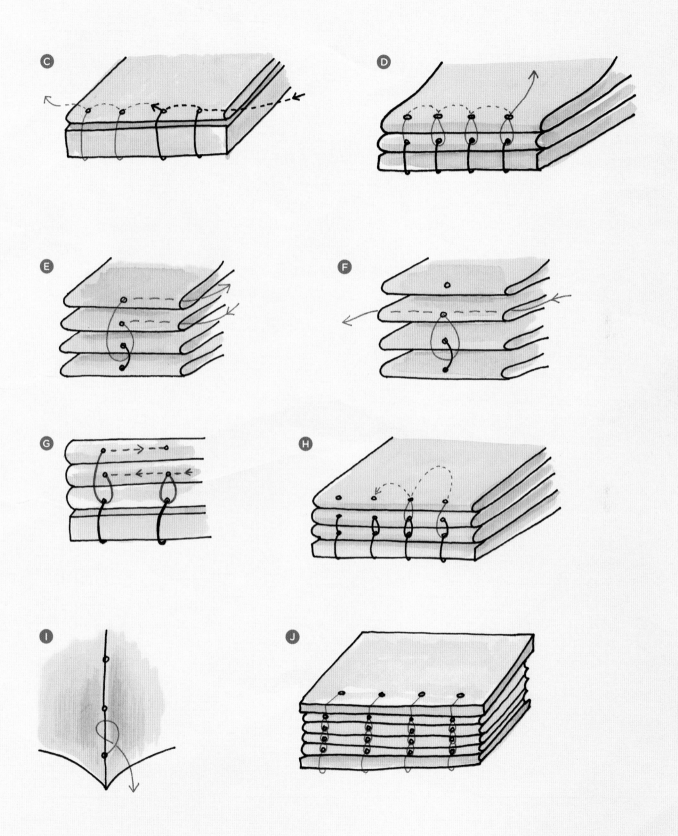

CREATIVE TECHNIQUES

DRAWING & JOURNALING

How can I talk about drawing without talking about my journals? They are intertwined and dependent on each other in ways I never predicted when I first learned the basics of bookmaking. Together they form the foundation of my work, a visual narrative that supports my interior and exterior worlds. I don't feel qualified to write in a scholarly way about drawing techniques, materials, or history. Nor can I say that my process is right for anyone else. I can only share with you how I came to this point. We all figure out what satisfies us from a combination of discipline and trust.

TOOLS AND MATERIALS

Mechanical pencils with eraser, one with soft lead and one with hard: I love mechanical pencils. I have a heavy hand when it comes to writing and mark making, and mechanical pencils help regulate the width and intensity of my marks. The contrast between thin and thick lines is important to me because it adds subtlety and depth to an image. Pencil is a primary material in my work for two reasons. First, it represents impermanence and vulnerability—with the swipe of an eraser it is gone. The second reason represents a central theme running throughout my work: honoring the common, everyday objects and moments in our lives. It's the small things that often bring the most joy.

Watercolor graphite pencil: This pencil allows you to extend the abilities of your traditional pencil when you want a more painterly effect.

Graphite stick: Basically a thick pencil without the outer wood casing, this is great for big lines and smudging.

Mars plastic eraser: This is my favorite eraser. Its white color means it never leaves a colored residue on your surface, unlike other erasers. It keeps its flexibility over

time and can be counted on to erase a wide range of marks—even ones that appear permanent. As with most erasers, it sometimes becomes coated with the material you are erasing. If this happens, I rub it against my apron or a rag, essentially erasing the top layer, and voilà—it's just like new!

Black and sepia artist pens in different widths: These are basically high-quality colored markers. The two most widely available brands are Faber-Castell Pitt Artist Pen and Pigma Micron. Since I have such a heavy hand I tend to use Faber-Castell pens because they have a stronger tip. A big plus with these markers is that, if you keep your hand moving, the ink doesn't bleed or seep through to the other side of your paper like some markers' inks do. They come in a range of widths, from extra-fine to brush tip. There is one thing to be aware of with all markers: if you are drawing over painted areas, make sure the painted surface is dry. Otherwise, the paint coats the tip of your marker and renders it useless. My impatience to work a surface has often led to double frustration—no mark and a ruined pen.

TECHNIQUES

"Drawing" sounds like an intimidatingly formal word for the marks and images I put down on paper. I've never had training in drawing or painting, but I came to both because of a natural meandering through materials and my ever-curious nature that insists on following my nose. Like so many others, I have suffered from the "I can't draw" syndrome that is born in childhood class-rooms. It's only when I started keeping a journal that I began to understand the power and joy of drawing.

Over the years I have started to keep many journals and sketchbooks, but each ended up abandoned and only one-fourth full. I wasn't motivated to sustain the routine or excited by what I saw on the paper. For one thing, the journals were written musings, mostly complaints and emotional outpourings of a dramatic nature—rather like examining my navel, feeling that it wasn't up to snuff, and observing how I was going to change that. Quite boring. The sketchbooks were places for preliminary drawings of works I had in mind or other ideas for future work. These drawings tended to be rough in nature and devoid of personality. Both journal and sketchbook were store-bought affairs, which made it even easier for me to abandon them as time went by, and they sat unopened on the shelf, keeping company with my previous attempts.

In the late 1990s I took a one-week class at North Carolina's Penland School of Crafts with Paulus Berensohn titled "Soul in Slow Motion." It was my first introduction to bookmaking and the absolute satis-faction that comes from constructing and using well this beloved functional object.

But it wasn't until I took a creative journaling class with Heather Allen Hietala (page 131), 10 years later, that it all came together for me. By this time I had the skills and knowledge to make my own journal, but I felt weighed down by figuring out what would be the "perfect" journal. Sometimes being a perfectionist can be helpful, but not in this case. So I bought a handmade journal from a friend that intuitively felt right: the size, the paper, the sturdy and practical Coptic binding. It wasn't an "aha" moment, just an easy certainty that this book fit my needs.

White gel pen and/or nib with acrylic ink: I'm always on the lookout for a pen that makes fine, opaque white marks over collage or paint. So far, the only two reliable products I have found are gel pens and acrylic ink used with a nib pen.

Red pen: I keep both a red fine-point permanent marker and a red extra-fine Pilot V Ball on my table. Again, this gives me the option of a thick or thin line, but each pen also has its own shade of red. I love these subtle differ-ences. Often it's the little details that really make a work special. Most red pens of this type are bad about bleeding through paper, so keep that in mind when using one. If a pen does bleed to the other side, I find a way to use that to my advantage.

Tortillion: Ⓐ A tortillion is a cylindrical drawing tool made from compressed fiber or rolled paper. I use it to blend pencil marks. A scrap of cotton knit fabric (like a piece of an old T-shirt) can work just as well unless you need fine detail. I have both on my table.

Because Heather's approach is really about discovering a journaling practice that suits the individual, I decided that there would be very few written words involved on the pages of my journal. I wasn't interested in my written thoughts, but in images, lines, and shapes—whatever I felt like putting down. This was to be an exercise in openness to what comes without an agenda, expectations, or editing. The usual suspects on my studio table—paper scraps, gouache, pencil, and glue stick—became the materials utilized. As the pages filled up I noticed several things: the journal was becoming very important to me; it held value; the images felt fresh, spontaneous, and exciting; the daily discipline of working in my journal became a grounding moment in the busy nature of my days. Over time I began to see the direct relationship between the images in my journal and the finished work in the studio. My journals contained the seeds of my work. By now they have become a personal history, a graphic memoir that explains who I am in a way words never could.

After I filled that handmade journal, I decided that I wanted to make subsequent ones myself. Although the overall dimensions and binding are consistent with that journal, I've experimented a lot with different types of paper. This is how I inadvertently learned about paper. Through drawing, painting, and collaging in my journal, I discovered the papers that worked best for my purposes both in and outside the journal. My journal also doubles as an accessible container for experimentation with materials and techniques. The first time I ever used gouache was in my journal, and it's a staple now. Confidence in my drawing ability came from the journals, too. It was only after looking back at early pages in my first journal that I realized their value. I saw spontaneity and life in those images, and that was exciting. It gave me the confidence to draw more. It took a bit of "distance" to see it. Often we are too close—we can't see the forest for the trees—or we judge too harshly up front. Time and distance are good teachers.

My journal is always on my studio table, and at some point in the day I pick it up. What I contribute that day comes in different ways, sometimes out of my head fully formed, as if I were only a conduit for an idea floating around out there. Other times it's slow going, maybe a scrap of paper strikes my fancy or reminds me of a dog's head, foot, or belly, and I pick up my pencil and start drawing.

I'd like to say I put something in my journal every day, but I don't. I average four or five days a week, although there have been stretches of weeks without anything added. At these times I often feel that I'm cheating myself. What have I lost by not getting it down? But the object of the journal isn't to produce guilt or pressure, so I turn that tape off and trust I'll get back to it. And I do.

My basic philosophy about my work in the studio and life in general is held in an image of a linear alphabet. You can't get from A to D without first going through B and C. Not that everything has to be linear, but we learn by walking through, not over or around. It's really the process, the movement (forward or backward) that interests me. I just want to keep learning.

PAINTING

I have never had any formal training in painting, so I have just experimented with techniques and materials. As with so much of my process, I figure it out as I go along. I think of myself as a dog following its nose, not quite sure where I'm headed, but I'm engaged and learning. The trail might lead to a tasty treat or a dead opossum (a tasty treat to some, I guess).

Oil paint is luscious and beguiling, but I learned early on that it wasn't for me. I'm too impatient to work with a material that takes days to dry. So naturally I gravitated toward water-based paint. Acrylic, gouache, and milk paint are now staples in my studio.

TOOLS AND MATERIALS

When it comes to materials, the adage "you get what you pay for" has been confirmed over and over again. The paint that has the strongest, truest colors and goes on the smoothest is the most expensive because of the concentration of pigment. I have a combination of both high- and mid-quality paints, but I stay away from the cheapest ones. Why fight with the materials when you don't need to? I've learned this the hard way.

Gouache in various colors: Gouache is similar to watercolor paint, but it's heavier in pigment and opaque rather than transparent. The opacity is what I love about gouache—it can look very solid and flat. I keep about 10 Winsor & Newton colors and mix them on a palette. The beauty of gouache is that even after it dries on your palette you can reactivate it with a wet brush. No waste!

Liquid acrylic paint in favorite colors: I prefer liquid acrylic over heavy-body acrylic when working on paper and collage. It goes on smoother, dries faster, and can be purchased in smaller quantities. Like paper, this is subject to personal choice. Either way, Golden paint (also known as Golden Artist Colors) is the best. I keep shades of red, brown, yellow, black, blue, and green on hand. I supplement this group with premixed colors by FolkArt purchased at craft supply stores.

Black and white gesso: Gesso is generally used as a base layer on canvas and wood, but I use it as my standard white and black. I love its opaque, matte finish and durability. Golden gesso is my top choice.

Milk paint: I could sing a love song to milk paint. It has qualities that are unique. It is a totally natural product, and the finish is hard, opaque, and very durable. Because it isn't petroleum or latex based, it renders a surface that doesn't feel plastic in any way (the one drawback to acrylic paint for me). I buy it from the Old Fashioned Milk Paint Company (see page 143). It comes in powder form, and you mix up only what you need at the moment because it has a short shelf life. The range of base colors is limited, but they can be mixed to extend that range. One of the beauties of milk paint is that you can apply layers of color and then sand through to reveal those layers. It also develops a beautiful dull shine—a natural finish—after being burnished. Milk paint also works well as a base layer for other paints, collage, and drawing. Just remember to always use a dust mask when mixing and sanding milk paint.

Paintbrushes in various sizes for paint and shellac:
I'm hard on brushes, so I keep a few mid-quality brushes and the rest low quality in both natural and synthetic bristles. Once I've worn these out I can easily replace them. I have three different containers of paintbrushes: one for all water-based paint except milk paint (milk paint makes your bristles separate), one for milk paint, and one for shellac. For shellac, I buy a couple of small, cheap natural bristle brushes. Once you use a brush for shellac it stays a shellac brush because it gets stiff. Also, shellac is an oil-based product, whereas everything else I use is water based. The two don't mix.

Acrylic ink in various colors: This is an acrylic-based permanent ink that is water resistant when dry. I use it for overdrawing and adding detail on collages and papier-mâché animals. I use a nib pen when drawing with this ink. Daler-Rowney FW Artists' Acrylic Ink is my favorite brand.

Nib pen or dip pen: I have a basic pen with a standard extra-fine nib. You can find these at art and craft supply stores. They generally come in a set.

Shellac: I use shellac as a subtle accent. Its brown, watery color also adds an aging effect to paper. I buy orange shellac flakes online (from www.woodcraft.com) and mix it with denatured alcohol to dissolve the flakes. This allows me to have a couple of jars of different strength shellac handy; a little goes a long way. In fact, when I order these flakes I try and split the order with a friend. Orange shellac has a slightly different color than the ready-mixed shellac you buy at hardware stores. Be aware of shellac's safety issues: use it in a well-ventilated area and always read the safety precautions on the label. It can be runny and a bit unpredictable when applied to paper. That's actually one of the things I love about it, but between that and its potentially toxic qualities, it may not be your cup of tea.

TECHNIQUES

I often use paint in my collages and drawings. At these times paint becomes just another material among several, not something unto itself. It's similar to pieces of colored paper and colored markers. Other times, paint is the sole material I use.

I like to paint on a hard, flat surface such as tin or wooden board. First I prepare and seal the surface. For board this involves three coats of gesso; for tin, a coat of paint with an adhesive mixed in (see page 42 for more on painting tin). From there I build the background by painting layers of colors. When dry, I sand back through to create depth. Once I have a colored surface to work on, I begin painting an image and go from there. If I don't like what I have painted, I get out the sandpaper and sand back part of the paint to reveal a new starting point (don't forget your dust mask!). Then I begin painting again until I'm satisfied with the outcome.

Painting papier-mâché is a bit different because often I like some of the newspaper text to show through. In that case, I thin down gesso or acrylic paint and use it as a wash to color the surface. From there I come in with full-strength liquid acrylics or milk paint to complete the design.

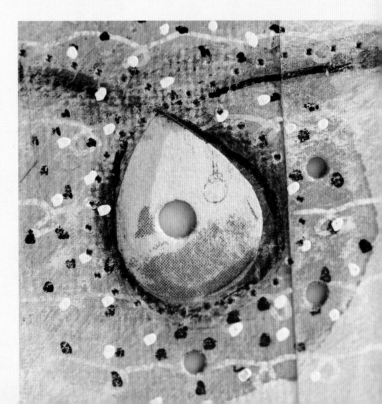

COLLAGE

Visitors to my studio are often surprised that I work across such a wide range of media. Although the imagery in my work is consistent, it's true that it's a diverse group of materials. One definition of collage is "a combination or collection of various things." That describes much of my work.

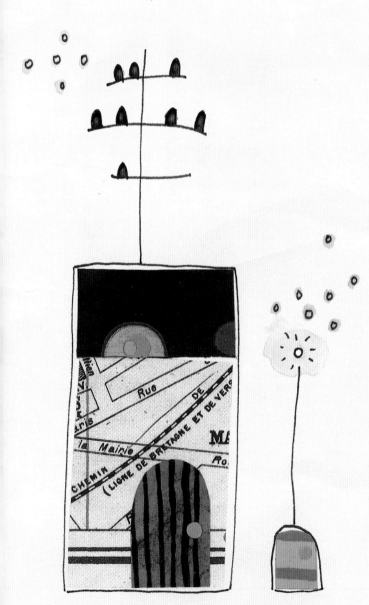

TOOLS AND MATERIALS

Materials for collage are more varied than the tools. In fact, most of these tools are probably already among your craft supplies.

Scissors: Cutting paper dulls scissors, so I have one pair of scissors for fabric and one pair for paper. Scissors are another tool that falls under the category "you get what you pay for." I've had the same two pairs of scissors for 25 years!

Craft knife: A utility knife has a difficult time making delicate cuts, so a craft knife works better for cutting single pieces of paper for collage.

Traditional hole punch: Ⓐ The diameter of a traditional hole punch is wider than the largest tip on the Japanese hole punch (page 14), so I keep both. I also have a couple of craft hole punches with even wider diameters.

Self-healing cutting mat: This is your surface to cut on when you use the craft knife. I recommend one that measures at least 18 x 24 inches (45.7 x 61 cm) so that it is useful for different size projects.

Glue stick: I love a good glue stick. My favorite is UHU Stic colored glue stick. It rubs on purple, so you can tell exactly where the glue is. Once the glue dries, the color disappears. For more information on glue sticks, see page 19.

Tortillion: A tortillion is a cylindrical drawing tool made from compressed fiber or rolled paper. I use it to blend pencil marks. A scrap of cotton knit fabric (like a piece of an old T-shirt) can work just as well unless you need fine detail. I have both on my table.

Ⓐ

TECHNIQUES

I mentioned earlier that I'm a collector of bits and pieces—anything that catches my eye, especially paper. Besides the sheets of decorative paper that I buy, I am constantly on the lookout for found paper of various types: tags, tickets, and paper with exciting patterns, colors, or textures. Because "one man's trash is another man's treasure," there's usually no shortage of freebies out there.

Collage is all about creating relationships between bits and pieces, relationships that make sense or not. I'm interested in possibilities: What happens when I put this together with that? Where does that combination lead? Is this a trigger for more possibilities or a dead end? Am I excited by what I see? Am I engaged? If not, why not? I'm not really thinking these thoughts on a conscious level when I'm working. For me it's an intuitive process, but if I had to put words to the process, I guess those would be the ones.

When I'm working on a collage I have the following materials available on my studio table: pencils, artist's pens, gouache, small bottles of liquid acrylic paint, hole punches, acrylic ink, a nib pen, scissors, shellac, a tortillion, an eraser, paintbrushes, a jar of water, a shallow bin full of scraps of paper, old letters, canceled postage stamps, and—of course—my trusty UHU Stic colored glue stick. Usually I start with a blank piece of Rives BFK paper (page 12) and glue down a chosen piece of paper. From there I draw, paint, and glue, responding and building from that initial piece of paper. Sometimes I have a general theme in mind, but usually it's following the thread of interest as I add and build. I try not to micromanage the process because accidents and smudges often enhance the piece and add depth. Or these mess-ups make you glue down something else to cover it up, and that creates something different, but just as exciting.

Here's a little story: At one point I had my studio at home in a tiny furnace room attached to the back of our house. The furnace needed to be replaced, and I had to vacate the studio for a few days. I covered or packed up my supplies so nothing would get damaged. Or at least I thought I had. Somehow a bin of my collage papers

became exposed and a small amount of water leaked on top of them. By the time I realized what had happened the papers were dry and the workmen gone. I figured I'd just throw out the papers, but when I started sorting through them I found a treasure—paper so much more interesting that the original. The water had caused some of the papers to bleed on others in random shapes and colors. This created depth and layers of subtle changes in color. They were so beautiful! That bin of "damaged" paper fed my work for months.

How do I know when to stop? Every once in a while this can be tricky, and I go overboard, but usually I intuitively know when it's done; I have a sense of satisfaction or pleasure. The wonderful thing about working in collage is that you can move shapes around before committing to the glue stick. So if I'm unsure about adding one more thing I can just lay it on the paper and move it around until I'm sure. That being said, I don't like everything I make. Often these pieces get recycled and repurposed into new work.

SEWING

There are some fancy home sewing machines out there now, but for everything in this book and for everything I make, only a basic machine is needed. In fact, one could make every project in this book with only hand-sewing. Granted, it would take longer, but it can be done and be very beautiful. Many times I choose to hand-sew instead of using the machine anyway, for the same reason that we are drawn to things made by hand: our hands impart humanity to whatever we create. It's this quality that breathes life into an object.

When using sewing as a design element, my approach is the same as for paper collage. Paper and fabric are interchangeable when considering pattern, color, and texture, the only difference being the inherent properties and limitations of each material.

Like decorative paper, I keep fabric in a range of colors on an open shelf in my studio. I like to have it visible rather than tucked away in a drawer. This helps me know what I have at a glance. Plus, it's exciting and inspiring to see the mix of fabrics next to each other. Alongside the yards of fabric are several bins containing scraps. These are for cutting and building images, just as I do with paper collage.

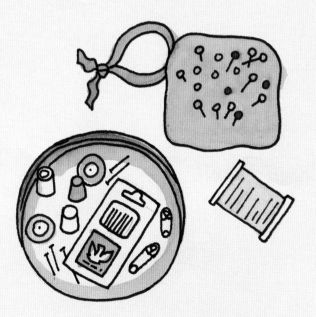

TOOLS AND MATERIALS

Right next to my main studio table is my sewing table. Here's what I keep handy.

Beeswax disk for waxing thread: This can be found in most fabric and crafts stores.

A bin of fabric scraps and strips

Felt: The best felt is true wool felt. It's stronger and has a depth of color and a feel that only natural fibers can give. It's hard to find locally in a range of colors, so I keep a few squares of the synthetic-blend felt that you can buy in fabric and craft stores. Because I only use it sparingly in small shapes, I can live with this compromise.

Fusible interfacing: I use this when I want a cloth book to have a stiff or rigid look and feel. You can use any mid- to heavy-weight fusible interfacing available at fabric stores, but I prefer to use fusible horsehair canvas interfacing for its superior flexibility and body. Although it used to contain actual horsehair strands, it is now a blend of natural and synthetic fibers. It is used in men's tailoring and as a backing for heavy needlework. It's available at specialty fabric stores and online.

Iron and ironing board

Pincushion with straight pins

A selection of cotton fabrics: Patterns and color are what draw me to a fabric. I use mostly cotton fabric because I can tear it easily and I like the soft effect of torn edges. Even so, I don't limit myself to cotton. My fabric shelf holds all types of fabric, including old clothes that have worn out but have an interesting print or represent memories I can't bear to part with. These can be incorporated into projects in a variety of ways. It only takes a small piece of a beloved garment to bring back those memories.

Sewing machine: My machine is an old Singer that my parents gave me years ago, which I'm attached to for sentimental reasons, but any machine will do. I use a

TEARING FABRIC

Cotton, silk, and some fine-wool fabric can be torn instead of cut with scissors or a rotary cutter. Tearing fabric leaves you with soft, slightly frayed edges. I love the subtle, blending effect of torn edges. Fabric is composed of threads going in one direction (the warp) woven with threads going in the other direction (the weft). This means that it has a grain running up and down and left and right. Fabric tears along a straight line (the grain) so you know your measurements remain the same from end to end. A bonus is that once you have removed loose threads resulting from the tearing process, the torn edges have a way of sealing the borders, thereby effectively eliminating any more fraying as long as it's not handled roughly or washed. (If you are making something that will be put in the washing machine, you will need to stitch the torn edges under or use a zigzag stitch to prevent fraying. The agitation of the washer and movement of the water loosen the border threads.)

To tear fabric, make a small cut ¼ to ½ inch (6 mm to 1.3 cm) long on one edge. Using both your hands, grab the edges of the fabric near the cut and pull evenly. You might have to give a short tug to get it started. Remove all loose threads from the edge. Repeat on all sides.

Note: It's hard to effectively tear strips of fabric less than ½ inch (1.3 cm) wide unless it is very finely woven fabric.

straight stitch mostly and occasionally a zigzag stitch when creating books. Even the most basic machines have these two stitches.

Sewing needles: I keep a range of sizes for hand-sewing everything from a single thread to six-ply embroidery floss.

Thread: I use Coats & Clark Dual Duty Plus All Purpose thread. Although I don't think it's the best thread, it is readily available and affordable.

TECHNIQUES

Because I approach sewing much like a collage technique, my process is similar. To begin, I gather a range of fabrics that might fit the idea I'm working on. This includes yardage as well as scraps. I choose a background piece of fabric and begin to build upon that. I cut shapes and play around with the composition, adding, taking away, sometimes removing everything and starting over. It's like working on a felt board because the fabric clings to itself. When I'm happy with the overall composition I draw a diagram or take a digital image I can refer back to. This helps especially if I have lots of layers and small shapes. If I get lost and can't remember what comes next, I check my diagram or photo. That being said, I leave the door open to fiddle with the sequence and composition as I go along; it's never set until all the pieces are sewn down.

Next I remove all the pieces and begin to machine- or hand-sew the shapes down, a layer at a time. I use straight pins to hold the layers together as I sew. This is especially helpful with round shapes because they can buckle as you sew around. Also, if using a machine, I set my machine stitch length at 6 to 7 stitches per inch (2.5 cm) (a basting stitch). This prevents the fabric from puckering when sewing through lots of layers. If I have a group of small shapes that are too small to pin in place, I dab the tiniest bit of my glue stick (page 19) on the back of the shape to keep it from moving while I'm sewing it down. I use glue sparingly because I want the overall piece to retain the suppleness of cloth. Fabric glue and fusible bonding products work well for layering, but your final product will be much stiffer.

For finishing I use basic hand-sewing stitches such as the running stitch Ⓐ and the hem stitch Ⓑ to add playful surface embellishment and provide stability to the overall piece.

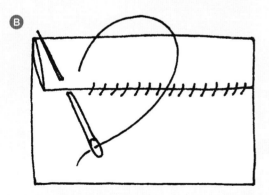

My Sewing Machine

My mother's sewing machine occupied a special place in our house. I was one of four girls, and when I was very young, Mother was often at the machine making dresses or costumes for one of us. I guess I was fascinated by her magic machine, because by age four I had learned the basics. I have vivid memories of the first piece of clothing I made from a pattern (a flowered terry swimsuit cover-up with bias tape trim) as well as the first thing I made from my imagination (a stuffed dog modeled after our stinky black Labrador retriever, Bebe). Not long after, my mother abandoned the sewing machine for a career as a ceramic artist, but I kept her machine humming all the way up to college, when my parents gave me the Singer I still use today. I made most of my own clothes through high school. Many a weekend night I would be home sewing instead of out with friends. I guess I was a sewing nerd.

Like my mother, I moved on from making clothes to other creative ventures, but unlike her, sewing is still central to my work. Whether it's a binding, decorative stitching on a cloth book, or stitches holding a handmade envelope closed, the influence of my mother's lessons with needle and thread are every-where. Even the dotted lines in many of my drawings look like stitches to me.

In all aspects of my life I am drawn to basic techniques, simple machinery, and readily accessible materials. From this foundation, exciting and intricate work can come to life using pattern, color, and placement. With the sewing machine I primarily rely on a basic straight stitch for everything. For some this might feel limiting, but for me it's the framework I use for endless possibilities. Plus, it adds an element of challenge that keeps me interested.

WORKING WITH PAPIER-MÂCHÉ, TIN, AND WIRE

PAPIER-MÂCHÉ

I started working with papier-mâché a few years ago. I wanted to make a 3-D dog out of some material that would be strong but easy to work with. Both clay and wood required special tools or equipment. The beauty of papier-mâché was that I already had everything I needed: flour, water, newspaper, and masking tape.

I started off by getting a book out of the library to figure out the basics. There are two basic methods to working with papier-mâché—layered paper (strips of paper layered on top of each other) or paper pulp (chewed-up paper used like modeling clay)—and several options for the binder. I knew that I wanted to use layered paper and that I wanted that paper to be newspaper. I like the ideas of repurposing my morning read and the visual effect of text and images that already exist on the paper peeking through on the animal's body. As far as a binder, it took some experimenting to figure out which one worked best for my purposes.

I began with flour and water heated to make a paste. I really liked this binder the best because the flour paste feels good in my hands, and the flour came right out of my cupboard—no trip to the store for supplies. As I began to make more animals and started selling my papier-mâché work, I ended up changing binders. The downside to flour paste is that bugs like it. Papier-mâché work—especially in warmer climates—can become nibbled on. This shouldn't be a problem if your project isn't meant to last or if it has several layers of acrylic paint over it, but I didn't want to worry or be restricted, so I changed binders. Other options are wallpaper paste or diluted PVA glue. I tried the glue, but I didn't like the feel of it. I ended up with wallpaper paste, and now that's my binder of choice. It's easy to mix up and lasts for weeks if covered. Below you will find recipes for flour and wallpaper paste binders and directions for the layering method. If you want to learn

more about papier-mâché, there are many more ways to work with papier-mâché than what I do. I recommend your local library or bookstore.

MY METHOD

Tear (rather than cut) newspaper into strips. Torn edges are fibrous, which makes them adhere easily as well as blend well with previous layers so you don't end up with visible seams. Tear with the grain for long, straight strips. I usually tear a full sheet of newspaper in half vertically (down the fold) and then in half again, but this time horizontally (on the crosswise fold). This means I start tearing strips from a quarter-size sheet. This strip size is easy to work with as you are layering.

Crumple up more newspaper to create the shape you want and use masking tape to hold the paper together. The tighter you crumple the paper, the firmer and heavier the foundation shape, which in turn creates a harder final shape.

Spread a layer of paste on the shape. Dip or spread paste on a paper strip and wrap it around the shape. Continue to coat strips of newspaper with paste and wrap them, keeping the strips smooth with no folds or buckles. Make three or four layers, going in different directions, all over the shape. Let dry. Then repeat layering the strips all over. Let dry again. If the shape is still flexible after it is completely dry, repeat layering again. Your final shape should be hard and feel solid.

Note: The drying process can take a while, especially if you live in a humid climate. To speed the process you can create a "hot box" or drying box with a cardboard box and a clip lamp. Just be sure not to leave the box unattended and monitor the temperature so that it doesn't get too hot and burn the paper or cardboard.

PAPIER-MÂCHÉ RECIPES

FLOUR PASTE

2 tablespoons (30 g) unbleached all-purpose flour

Approximately 1 cup (235 ml) cold water

Add the flour and $1/2$ cup (120 ml) of the water to a small bowl. Whisk until blended and no lumps remain. Pour into a small saucepan. Add a little less than an additional $2/3$ cup (160 ml) cold water and blend well. Turn the heat to medium-low and stir the mixture constantly until it thickens. Let cool, and you are ready to go. Store in an airtight container in the refrigerator when you're not using it.

WALLPAPER PASTE

2 tablespoons (30 g) wallpaper paste powder

2 cups (470 ml) warm water

In a medium bowl, mix the wallpaper powder and water with a whisk until blended. Let sit for 20 minutes. If there are any lumps, whisk a bit more. It should be a bit thicker than heavy cream; if it's too thick, add water, a little at a time, to achieve the right consistency. If it's too thin, add 1 teaspoon (5 g) powder and whisk again. Let sit for another 20 minutes and stir again. Store in an airtight container in a cool place. You know it's old and no longer good when it gets watery.

TIN

Tin as we know it today is actually tin-plated steel—steel for strength and tin to resist rust and corrosion. Whether you use cans or boxes, something new or old, the potential of tin is downright exciting. But figuring out how to handle tin with ease can take a while. Although tin is a common material found in a wide range of shapes, working with it is not quite as simple as some books make it out to be. (The books I used had no images of adhesive bandages or ragged metal edges!) But the reality is that tin is easy to work with, once you understand its nature. It's the same for all materials—there's always a learning curve.

With Bobby Hansson's book, *The Fine Art of the Tin Can*, in hand, I started experimenting. It was a frustrating experience because using tin is so different than working with either paper or fabric. When learning to work with a new material, I often need a hands-on demo—especially when I'm dealing with a material that can fight back. (A tin scrap can cut your hand faster than you'd expect.) All I wanted were a few basics, so I started looking for a short class to take. I found one at Penland with Ellen Wiske and another several years later, again at Penland, this time with Bobby Hansson himself. Both Bobby and Ellen are great teachers. I learned the basics I needed with Ellen, and Bobby was the icing on the cake. (He's also quite the character!)

Since taking Ellen's class, tin has become a regular in my bag of tricks. Sometimes I use the existing shape of the tin object, and other times I deconstruct it so that I can use the tin in a different format. For the past few years I have been painting on tin. I used to haunt secondhand stores for tin trays and large cans that, when flattened, would yield a large area for working. I liked painting on top of a surface that already had history and color, but I began to use so much tin that it became easier and cheaper to buy a roll of galvanized steel flashing at the hardware store, which comes in different widths and lengths, and cut it down to the size and shape I wanted. Preparing the surface for painting requires a bit more prep time, but I figure it evens out considering the time and energy I saved not having to hunt for tin trays. And my elbow grease puts my own history on the piece.

WORKING WITH TIN

There are two different approaches to working with tin: hot or cold connections. Soldering and the use of any type of heat to join tin with tin or other objects is a hot connection. Cold connections involve rivets, tabs, rings, grommets, wire, or chains—any joining technique that doesn't involve heat.

Through experimentation I gravitated toward working only with cold connections, which appealed to my low-tech approach to materials. It often feels like a game to me: how can I make this connect with that? Imagine not being able to use glue to join wood or paper—same idea. That kind of problem solving is either fun or irritating, depending on your nature.

Using tin in the basic ways I do for the projects in this book is easy once you get the hang of cutting it. If you really get the bug to expand your knowledge base with tin, I recommend finding a class or workshop. These types of classes are usually held in a metals studio with lots of tools, specialized equipment, and a good ventilation system. It's more bang for your buck and shortens the learning curve.

BASIC TOOLS AND MATERIALS

Awl for punching holes

Bench block (a flat piece of steel for flattening tin)

Can opener

Dapping block for shaping tin: Mine is fashioned from a tree stump (see page 113), but you can also use a wooden salad bowl.

Earplugs

Eyelet tool with eyelets: These are handy for fastening and sealing edges.

Flat- and round-nosed jeweler's pliers

Galvanized steel flashing: This comes in either flat sheets or long rolls. If you aren't sure how much you will be working with, start with a sheet first; it's more economical in the long run.

Gloves: These are a must for working with tin. I use Atlas 370 gloves because they fit like a second skin, allowing for good dexterity while enhancing strength and protection for your skin. The nitrile-coated palms and fingertips keep materials from slipping in your hands.

Green scrubbie: I use a simple dish scrubber for preparing surfaces for painting.

Grommet tool with grommets: Like the eyelet tool with eyelets, these are for fastening and sealing edges.

Hammers: I use a flat head hammer, a round head hammer, and a rubber mallet depending on the task.

Metal files (for smoothing out burrs or rough edges)

Nail set (for widening holes)

Needle tool (for punching holes)

Packing tape: Tape can protect existing images on tin while you are working.

Permanent marker

Safety glasses

Sandpaper: A must for preparing a surface for painting. I keep 60 grit, 100 grit, and 120 grit on hand.

Steel wool (coarse and medium): Perfect for when you need something stronger than a green scrubbie for preparing a surface for painting.

Tin cans, trays, or decorative tins

Tin snips for cutting tin

Wire, various gauges

CUTTING TIN

I use gloves (see above) when I'm working with tin, especially when cutting. No matter how careful I am, without gloves I always seem to cut myself, often without even realizing it until I see drops of red. It's helpful to know up front that cutting tin isn't like cutting paper in either the action or the finished product. Your range of movement with the snips isn't as great, and the cut edges are too sharp or rough to stand alone.

DECONSTRUCTING A CAN

It's a good idea to save a few cans headed to the recycling bin and spend some time getting used to cutting tin. It feels awkward at first. Start by using a can opener to open both ends. Find the seam line on the can. Using tin snips, start at one open end and cut down alongside the seam line. You will need to gently bend one side of the cut upward as you go along to be able to move down the can. It's easy to dent or even tear the can as you cut if you aren't careful. I try to move slowly but steadily as I cut. If you find you can't cut all the way from one end to the other, then cut as far as possible and start again from the other end. You will probably end up with a jagged edge; that's to be expected. There will be a band at the top and the bottom of the can. These need to be cut off. (You can buy a can opener that opens the end and removes the band at the same time, which means one less step.)

As you cut around the can to remove the bands, bend the band up and away so that it can't cut you. Once the bands are removed, trim all the jagged edges. The can is still in a round shape. To flatten it, put one edge of the can on a bench block or flat hardwood board and slowly hammer it flat with a rubber mallet. Continue to slowly work your way around the can. If you go too fast, the metal will buckle. Many cans have ridges around the sides; these will flatten out as you hammer. Once the metal is flat, you can use a flat-head hammer to continue to smooth any areas that are still ridged.

Safety note: Hammering tin can be quite loud and piercing, especially if you are hammering on a bench block with a metal hammer. I keep a pair of earplugs handy and use them faithfully. Safety glasses are also good practice when working with tin.

Once you have a flat piece of tin, use a permanent marker to draw the shape you want to cut out. Keep it simple at first. Start by cutting out the general shape, not along the line you drew. Once you have the general shape it's easier to move the tin while you cut along the exact line. As you cut, move the trimming up and away from the cut. I have found that it's hard to trim little bits; it's easier to trim areas in a broad way. Make sure you have a trash can or recycling bin close so that all scraps are quickly put into the bin. Otherwise—ouch!

Use a metal file to remove all burrs and smooth out the edges. File in only one direction so your file stays sharp. I usually file at a slight angle on each side and then across the top of the edge. I try to smooth it out and dull the edge at the same time.

SHAPING TIN

Shaping tin is done in two different ways, either by hammering or by using a pneumatic device with die blocks to create specific shapes. Simple as I am, I use a round-head hammer and something called a dapping block. Dapping blocks allow sheet metal to be formed into domes and other uniform shapes with ease. They come in wood and hardened metal with different size depressions on the same block. For the projects in this book, I used an oversize homemade wooden dapping block. It's an old tree stump that has three rounded

depressions of varying depths. A friend made it for me with a chainsaw and a seasoned stump. Before I had the stump dapping block, I used a thick wooden salad bowl I bought at a yard sale.

When shaping tin, or any sheet metal, the key is to do it gradually; otherwise, the metal will buckle and fold. Once that happens it's hard to reverse the buckle and almost impossible to reverse a fold. Using a round-head hammer, start on the outside edge of the tin sheet placed in the shallowest depression. Hammer as you move the tin around and around the depression. You will begin to see it change shape. As this happens, gradually move the tin into the middle of the depression. Once you have shaped the tin so it fits well in that depression, move to the next deepest depression and repeat the process until you reach the shape you want.

Having the appropriate hammer is important to achieve the desired surface. A round-head hammer creates a smooth surface. Ball-peen hammers create a dimpled surface.

PAINTING TIN

Prepping the surface is essential with tin if you want to paint it. The two basic preparation goals are degreasing and creating a tooth (or roughness) so the paint can bond to the metal. This needs to be done even if you are using a recycled tin and the surface is already commercially painted. You might not need to do as much sanding, but you still need to dull the surface.

Here is my sequence:

1. Sand the surface with 60-grit sandpaper.

2. Sand with 120-grit sandpaper.

3. Wash and scrub well with a green scrubbie and dish detergent.

4. Dry thoroughly.

Now you are ready to paint. Spray paint can be applied directly and it will bond well. Acrylic paint often needs an added bonding agent, as does milk paint. I use a base coat of milk paint mixed with Extra Bond, a nontoxic polymer emulsion that allows milk paint to adhere to nonporous surfaces (see resources on page 143). Further coats don't need Extra Bond, and acrylic paint can be applied over milk paint. I like to put several coats of different colors on, then sand back to reveal the layers. Painted surfaces also make a good background for collage.

WIRE

Wire and tin go well together. Made from similar materials with similar properties as tin, wire can be used to join as well as provide a finishing element for tin work. Using it to edge tin also reduces sharp edges and makes your work easier to handle. I like to keep a range of wire gauges and colors in the studio, just like I do with linen thread for binding books. A handy fact: the larger the gauge, the thinner the wire.

Binding wire, also known as bailing wire, is my preferred wire for armature, crown frames (page 115), and edging. It can be found at seed and feed stores and some hardware stores. It comes in 14 or 16 gauge and is usually oiled to keep it from rusting.

Colored wire in 24 and 26 gauge can be found at hardware and craft stores. I treat this gauge wire as thread. "Sewing" with wire is both functional and decorative.

BASIC WIRE TOOLS

Flat-nosed jeweler's pliers

Gloves: I always use Atlas 370 gloves when working with binding wire. The coated palms help me grip the wire securely and keep the wire from cutting into my skin when I pull it tight. Smaller-gauge wire is easier to handle without gloves, except when you need to pull an area tight.

Metal file

Round-nose jeweler's pliers

Flush cutters (a type of wire cutters): I recommend a pair that is 4½ or 5 inches (11.4 or 12.7 cm).

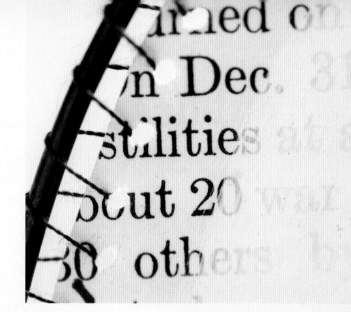

ABOUT WIRE

Most wire that you buy in hardware and craft stores is annealed. That means it has gone through a process involving heat that makes it "softer," or easier to work with. As you bend and manipulate annealed wire it becomes stiffer or "work hardened." For example, when I'm using binding wire to make the armature of a crown, there are only so many times I can bend and twist the wire before it becomes so stiff I'm unable to manipulate it even with the aid of tools. This property doesn't usually create problems; in fact, it's an advantage in most cases because the wire hardens, thereby providing a more stable structure. But it's good to know the limitations of your materials.

Wire usually comes in rolls or bound around a spool. Sometimes when you unwind it off the spool it has bends and kinks. These can be straightened out with flat-nose pliers. Flat-nose pliers are also good for gripping and making right angles. Round-nose pliers are used to create circles and spirals. By gripping one end of a piece of wire and bending it over the round nose, a smooth curve is formed.

If I'm using a larger gauge wire, such as the binding wire, I like to finish all ends by filing to a blunt point. This creates a nice visual transition rather than an abrupt finish and also makes it easier for ends to be tucked behind other wires when you want to conceal the end point. Always file in one direction to keep your file from becoming dull.

CONVENTIONAL BOOKS

BOOK CARD

Creating small collages or drawings is similar to creating a journal entry for me. I get the chance to play and explore with the materials on my studio table. These casual endeavors often lead to fresh and exciting ideas for more developed works. Plus, it is my belief that one of life's pleasures is the surprise of finding a handmade greeting in your mailbox—and a mini-book is even more fun than a card!

MAKE

1. Decide on the dimensions of the book. The one shown here is 3 x 2 inches (7.6 x 5.1 cm). Cut two pieces of board to this size using a craft knife and ruler. The grain should be going in the same direction as the spine.

2. Cut two pieces of decorative paper ½ inch (1.3 cm) larger than your cover dimensions; mine are 3½ x 2½ inches (8.9 x 6.4 cm). You have a choice here for the grain—it can either be with or against the grain of the board. Whichever you choose, the cover and the text paper must be the same direction so that your cover does not warp. **Ⓐ**

3. One at a time, glue the boards to the cover paper with book glue. Follow the instructions for Making a Book Cover (page 22). Make sure both boards sit under a weight for at least an hour.

4. Cut the text paper. To figure out your dimensions, subtract ¼ inch (6 mm) from the cover length and multiply the width times the number of folds. I generally have either five or seven folds in my book cards— a book with five folds has six pages, and a book with seven folds has eight pages. You should have an uneven number of folds so that the first and last page open into the book. My text paper here measures 18 x 1¾ inches (45.7 x 4.4 cm) for five folds. You will also need to be aware of grain—it should match the direction of the cover paper.

NOTE: I find it easiest to cut a long strip equal to the width less ¼ inch (6 mm), without measuring the length at this point. Once I have made the folds I lightly mark the end with a pencil. I line the pencil mark up with a straight line on my self-healing mat and cut it with a ruler and

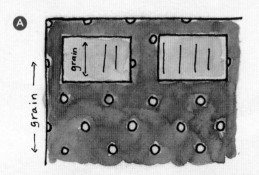

GATHER

Basic Bookmaking Tool Kit (page 13)

Book board, 8 x 10 inches (20.3 x 25.4 cm): This can be Davey board or homemade book board (page 17); homemade board works well here because a thin board is best. Make sure the direction of the grain is marked.

Decorative paper, 8 x 10 inches (20.3 x 25.4 cm), for the covers, plus a few scraps for the collage

Text paper, 8 x 20 inches (20.3 x 50.8 cm): You can use anything that is long enough for the accordion folds, as long as it is not too light or too heavy; otherwise, it can't be folded and won't maintain its shape.

Weight (page 18)

Damp rag for wiping off excess glue

Waxed paper

Drawing, painting, and/or collage supplies, for the cover (see Creative Techniques, page 28)

String or linen cord, for closure (optional)

2 envelopes, handmade or store-bought

craft knife. This gives you some wiggle room in case you don't get your folds exactly the same—it takes practice to be able to make consistent folds. Make a light pencil mark on the front of your strip at one of the corners so you will know it's the front. You can erase this mark when you are done.

5. Lift up the weight and remove the covers.

6. With your front cover facing down, place the unfolded text paper strip on the back of your front cover from left to right. Position it evenly on three sides with the width extending past the right side. Ⓑ Gently fold the strip back to the left to match the text paper position of the other three sides. Now you have your "page" size.

7. Remove the strip from the cover and place it on your mat. Set the fold you just made by using your bone folder, making sure that the top and bottom

edges are parallel with the first page. Repeat the folding and setting process until you have the desired number of folds.

8. Glue the first and last pages to the covers with book glue. Place the front and back cover face down, with the front cover to the left and back cover to the right. On the back of your folded text-paper strip, carefully glue up the first page, being sure not to get glue past the fold. Ⓒ This can be a bit tricky until you get the hang of it, so take your time.

9. Turn the strip over and position it evenly on the front cover. Crease it with the bone folder, gently but firmly, making sure that the folded edge is completely glued down. Be sure to remove any excess glue with a damp rag—you don't want your book glued shut!

10. Repeat the gluing process for the last page and the back cover. Close the book and put it under a weight for at least two hours. It's a good idea to add waxed paper between the folds while under the weight if you went a bit too heavy with the glue.

11. Decorate the covers with drawings, paint, or collage. You can add a length of string or linen cord for a closure, if desired.

12. Now you can fill out the book and send it! Ⓓ

NOTE: For a nice finishing touch, you can use handmade or commercial envelopes to mail your books. I generally use two envelopes when I'm mailing my book cards—a small one to hold the book card and a larger one that satisfies the postal service's dimension requirements. This also gives your book extra protection as it travels.

SMALL ACCORDION STORYBOOK WITH CLOTH BAG

The format of the accordion fold lends itself to storytelling. The ability to see the story "unfold" without turning a page makes for a unique and fun viewer/reader experience. I enjoy creating small stories, or as I like to think of them, vignettes on the folds of accordion books. This is essentially an expanded version of the Book Card (page 46), with the addition of a handmade cloth bag to hold the finished storybook. Books are interactive and intimate—there is action involved, and it's often just between the reader and the book. The cloth bag extends that experience, while also enhancing the visual impact of the story contained inside.

MAKE

THE BOOK

1. Decide on the dimensions of your book. The one shown is 3 x 2½ inches (7.6 x 6.4 cm). Fold and tear a long strip of text paper the width of your book—note the grain direction so that it will match the grain of the board and cover paper.

2. Fold an accordion page (see page 20) to the correct width dimension. Score and tear off any excess length. My storybooks typically have three or five folds.

3. Draw, paint, or collage a story on the front folds. You can also continue the story on the back if you'd like. I usually use the front for the story and the back for my signature, date, and a small drawing that relates to the front pages. This way the book can be displayed open with the entire story visible. Ⓐ

NOTE: Spray the "accordion" with workable fixative if you have used pencil or gouache. This allows you to use your bone folder over the drawing without smudging when you are gluing the covers.

4. Cut two covers slightly larger than the dimensions of your text paper from lightweight book board. I say "slightly larger" because, as opposed to board that is ⅛ inch (3 mm) larger on each side as in the Book Card (page 46), here you don't want that overlap. This allows the book to have enough stability to stand open indefi-

Basic Bookmaking Tool Kit (page 13)

Book board, 8 x 10 inches (20.3 x 25.4 cm): This can be Davey board or homemade book board (page 17); homemade board works well here because a thin board is best. Make sure the direction of the grain is marked.

Decorative paper, 8 x 10 inches (20.3 x 25.4 cm), for the covers plus a few scraps for the collage

Text paper, 8 x 14 inches (20.3 x 35.6 cm): You can use anything that is long enough for the accordion folds, as long as it is not too light or too heavy; otherwise, it can't be folded and won't maintain its shape.

Drawing, painting, and/or collage supplies (see Creative Techniques, page 28)

Spray fixative (optional)

Weight (page 18)

Damp rag for wiping off excess glue

Waxed paper

¼ yard (22.9 cm) of cotton fabric for the cloth bag

Fabric scraps for embellishing the cloth bag

Sewing machine: For this project I used a sewing machine to sew the cloth bag, but hand-sewing works just as well if you don't have a machine.

Sewing needle

Thread

Straight pins

Embroidery floss (optional)

Small buttons (optional)

Ⓐ

nitely without the text paper sagging. Remember to make sure the grain of the board matches your text paper as well as the decorative cover paper.

5. Cut two pieces of decorative paper ¼ inch (6 mm) larger than the cover dimensions on all sides. You have a choice here for the grain—it can either be with or against the grain of the board. Whichever you choose, the grain of the cover and the text paper must be the same direction or your cover will warp.

6. One at a time, glue the boards to the cover paper with book glue. Follow the instructions for Making a Book Cover (page 22). Make sure both boards sit under a weight for at least an hour.

7. Place the front and back covers face down, with the front cover to the left and the back cover to the right. On the back of your folded text-paper strip, carefully glue up the first "page," being sure not to get glue past the fold. This can be a bit tricky until you get the hang of it, so take your time.

8. Turn the strip over and position it evenly on the front cover. Smooth it with the bone folder, gently but firmly, making sure that the folded edge is completely glued down. Be sure to remove any excess glue with a damp rag—you don't want your book glued shut!

9. Repeat the gluing process for the last page and the back cover. Close the book and put it under a weight for at least two hours. It's a good idea to add waxed paper between the folds while it's under the weight if you went a bit too heavy with the glue.

10. Decorate the covers if desired. I usually put something small on both the front and the back that reflects the story inside, but otherwise I leave it fairly plain because I like the contrast between the quiet cover and the busyness of the cloth bag and the inside of the book.

THE CLOTH BAG

1. Pick out fabric that complements the book. Decide whether you want your book to go in the bag vertically or horizontally. Note the width and length dimensions.

2. Cut or tear a piece of fabric that measures the width of the book plus 1 inch (2.5 cm) and twice the length plus ½ inch (1.3 cm). **B**

3. Cut scraps of fabric for embellishing the front of the bag.

4. Hand- or machine-sew embellishments onto the front. **C**

5. Fold the bag in half crosswise, wrong sides together, and pin. Machine- or hand-sew the two long sides ¼ inch (6 mm) from the torn edge, leaving the top side open.

6. Cut or tear a strip of fabric for a handle.

7. Tack on the handle by hand or machine. This can be done with thread using a simple straight stitch or by using a decorative stitch with embroidery floss. Small buttons can be added to hide the stitching, if desired. You can now slide the storybook into the bag.

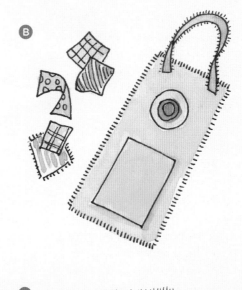

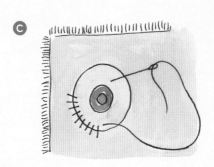

Trying to come up with ideas for stories can be daunting if you think about it too hard. Sometimes ideas don't come to me out of the blue, and I'm forced to create them while sitting at my studio table (usually with a deadline looming). How do I create something under pressure? Often I depend on my journals for the seeds of an idea. I flip through my journals and find an image that grabs me. Sitting at my studio table with collage and paint materials in front of me, I start with this image in mind and put something down on the page. I respond to what I just put down and continue building on the story in that way—before long, there is cohesiveness to the images. This is a matter of trust, because I don't know where I'm going, only that I'm heading somewhere. Every once in a while I come up with something I don't like, but generally I'm excited by the result—even more so when I realize this story exists simply because I stuck with it. Turn judgment off and trust your intuition!

How did you come to books? Making art feels like playing to me, possibly because I started doing it as a very young child under absolutely no pressure. Then, during art school, the playful aspect dimmed and the making of art felt serious and earnest. Particularly painful for me was the Finding of Worthy and Artistic Subject Matter. When I discovered artists' books in the 1990s, I felt great relief. I loved how the subject matter was wildly various and wacky. Because artists' books felt playful and not so serious, when I ventured into making them, I didn't worry about subject matter—I just made my books about whatever I was interested in at the time. I quit worrying and got back to playing and sketching, my two favorite activities finally brought together.

Interestingly, this new relaxation spread to my printmaking as well as to my drawing. It became possible to make prints, drawings, books, and even painted sculptural forms without the crippling seriousness and worry about subject matter.

Describe your creative process. My most recent series of work is a good example of my process of art making. It had its genesis in a conversation that I had with a friend a few years ago in which we realized that we had lived in the exact same small neighborhood in New Orleans many years before. It wasn't long before we were drawing large colored maps for each other to explain our favorite places in the labyrinthine inner life of the neighborhood, a place of ancient tribal divisions, prehistoric customs, and a blending of cultures.

Faubourg Nan Main Bon Dieu, Gwen Diehn and Laura Ladendorf
PHOTOGRAPH BY PHILIP DIEHN

We decided to collaborate on a series of work about the neighborhood. To begin, we each developed a large woodcut about aspects of the neighborhood. We came together every two weeks for almost a year to reflect on what we were doing separately and to see how it connected to each other's work.

We decided to bring our woodcuts together in a piece that would celebrate the inner and outer life of the neighborhood. This time we made an editioned book, a two-sided accordion housed inside a gatefold, a reference to the many gates in the place. I made paper from the bark of a willow tree in reference to the willow trees in the neighborhood. We made the gate out of milk-painted book board and closed it with a chicken bone.

The most recent evolution of the series, for me, has been making structures that are more sculptural than book-like, although they open and can be manipulated. All the pieces will be housed in a box that opens out to become a game-board-like neighborhood map. Playing with the piece will be yet another reference to playing in the streets of the neighborhood.

Faubourg Nan Main Bon Dieu, Gwen Diehn
PHOTOGRAPH BY PHILIP DIEHN

Faubourg Nan Main Bon Dieu, Gwen Diehn and Laura Ladendorf
PHOTOGRAPH BY PHILIP DIEHN

MATCHBOX BOOK

I have always been fascinated by boxes, especially small ones. They are just like books in a way—it's all about action and discovery. This project takes off on that theme while combining three things near and dear to my heart: repurposing materials headed for the landfill, creating objects that I can give to friends, and playing with materials.

MAKE

THE MATCHBOX

1. Very gently deconstruct both the matchbox cover and the box. This takes a bit of patience with the box. Once I am able to get the inside end flap up, I use my fettling knife to help release the side flanges. **A**

2. Decide what paper you want to use for the cover and the box. It can be the same paper for both or different papers for each.

3. Lay both the opened cover and the box down on your decorative paper and carefully trace around the outside of each. **B**

GATHER

Basic Bookmaking Tool Kit
(page 13)

Decorative paper, 8 x 10 inches
(20.3 x 25.4 cm), for wrapping
the matchbox

Text paper, 8½ x 11 inches
(21.6 x 28 cm)

Card stock, scrap paper, or a
small sheet of acetate for making a
template (you can also cut away the
sides of a clear lettuce box from
the grocery store and use the flat
part for a template)

Scrap paper for hole-making
template (page 23)

Empty matchbox, approximately
2 x 1½ inches (5.1 x 3.8 cm)

Damp rag for cleaning
excess glue

Old phone book

12 inches (30.5 cm) of 3- or 4-ply
linen thread

Sewing needle

Embellishments and decorations
(optional)

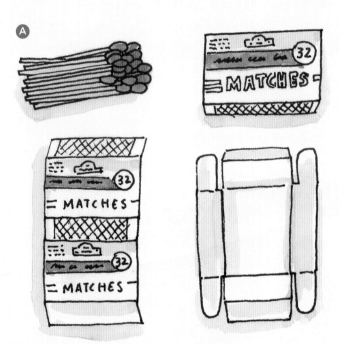

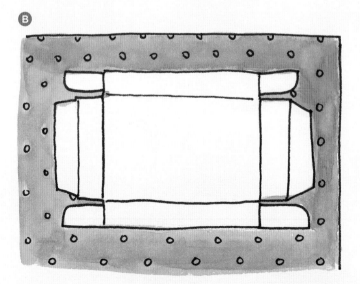

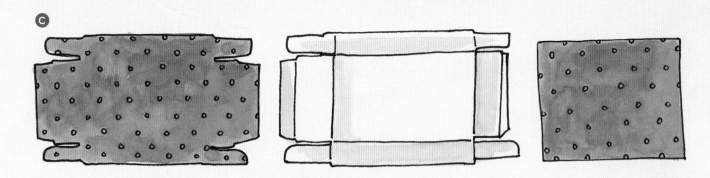

4. For the inside of the box you will need to cut a separate piece of paper. To figure out these dimensions, measure the inside of the box's bottom plus both long sides (for me that was 2⅛ x 2 inches [5.4 x 5 cm]) then add ¼ inch (6 mm) to the length (up-down) measurement (so mine became 2⅛ x 2¼ inches [5.4 x 5.7 cm]). The extra ¼ inch (6 mm) in length is used to wrap the paper over the edges of the sides. **C**

NOTE: You can make a template for the three pieces if you plan on creating a lot of these. You will still need to deconstruct the cover and box, but a template makes it easier to cut out multiples. Just trace the cover, box, and inside box dimensions (after you add the ¼ inch [6 mm]) onto card stock or acetate and cut them out. Acetate or a see-through template allows you to easily position the paper to take advantage of a pattern if you are using patterned paper.

5. Using a glue stick, apply glue on the back of the cover paper and glue it onto the open cover. Use the bone folder to remove air bubbles. Trim off any excess paper.

6. Using a glue stick, glue the paper for the inside of the box in place, positioning the paper so there is a ⅛-inch (3 mm) overhang on the top and bottom. Fold the extra bit of paper over the edge to the back of the box. Use the bone folder to crease it. **D**

7. Glue paper to the outside of the flattened box. Crease it with the bone folder. Trim off any excess paper.

8. Apply straight PVA glue (see page 19) for a faster bond on the inside flanges and flaps of the box. Fold the box back together and hold it in place with your fingers until the glue is set. It doesn't take very long for the glue to set, but once you remove your fingers, let the box sit for 10 to 15 minutes before putting any stress or pressure on it. I glue one end of the box at a time and use a damp rag to wipe up any excess glue on the box edges and my hands. **E**

9. Brush PVA glue on the inside flap of the cover and reseal it. Hold the pieces together with your fingers until the glue is set.

10. Once the box and cover are dry, make sure they slide from side to side easily.

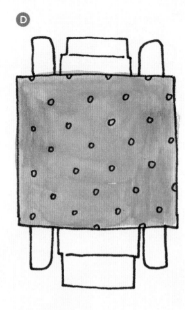

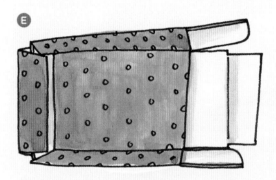

THE BOOK

1. Decide on the dimensions you want for your book. In the example here, I created one that measures 1½ x 1 inch (3.8 x 2.5 cm). You can adjust the size, as long as the finished book fits into the box with enough room around it to be easily removed.

2. Cut the text paper. I generally use three or four sheets that are folded in half to make a 12- or 16-page book; for this project, the cut paper measures 3 x 1 inch (7.6 x 2.5 cm) before folding.

3. Cut the cover paper ⅛ inch (3 mm) or so larger in width to allow for the folded text paper (mine was 3⅛ x 1 inch [7.9 x 2.5 cm]).

4. Fold the cover and text paper in half.

5. From scrap paper, make a template for a three-hole pamphlet stitch (page 23). Adjust the template size to fit this book (mine was about 1 x 1 inch [2.5 x 2.5 cm]).

6. Working in an old phone book, line up the fold of your template with the fold of the text paper and the cover. Use the template as your guide and punch three sewing stations with the needle tool.

7. Bind the book with a three-hole pamphlet stitch (page 24) using 1 ply of linen thread and a sewing needle. To get single-ply thread, untwist a short length of 3- or 4-ply linen thread, separating the individual plies or strands.

8. Decorate as desired.

REPURPOSED SURFACE NOTEBOOK

A pile of old wooden furniture on the side of the road, a box of odds and ends bound for the dumpster, a stack of paper waiting to be recycled—all these things get my imagination running with ideas of how to recreate, refashion, and reuse. Paper bags are a perfect example of a material that pulls me in. They are so practical and straightforward in their primary use, but that heavy brown paper seems meant for more life long after the groceries have been unloaded. Here's a technique I developed to create heavy, durable paper that can be used for both the covers and pages of a book while also recycling papers of all kinds. The binding is a simple basting stitch on the sewing machine, but a pamphlet stitch (page 24) would work just as well.

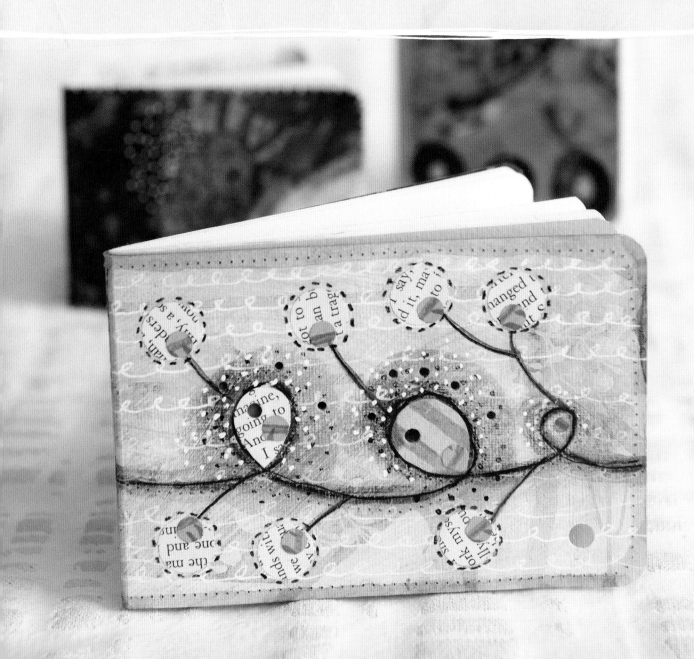

MAKE

1. Deconstruct the paper bag by pulling it apart at the glued edges. Try to tear it as little as possible.

2. Using scissors, trim off the raw glued edges of the side and bottom of the bag. Ⓐ

3. Using thinner book glue (page 19), glue decorative paper, book pages, or used copier paper to one side of the bag and then the other, being sure not to leave gaps—you don't want to see the bag showing through. It's important to do a thorough job of gluing so that there aren't air bubbles between the bag and the paper. Use your bone folder to smooth out the paper. Ⓑ

NOTE: You do not need to worry about grain in this project because you are layering the paper in different directions on both sides of the bag and adding layers of paint in the next steps. The layering of materials on both sides builds up the paper so that it doesn't warp.

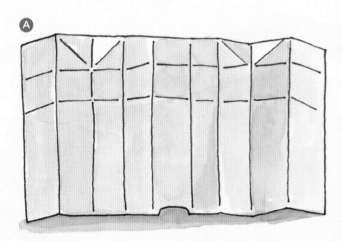

Ⓐ

Ⓑ

GATHER

Basic Bookmaking Tool Kit (page 13) with thinner book glue (page 19)

Brown paper bag

Other paper for laminating (gluing) onto the brown bag, enough to create two or three layers on top: This can be decorative papers you are ready to pass on, old book pages, copies from the recycling bin—almost any midweight paper; tissue-weight paper is hard to glue, and heavy paper is hard to fold. Keep in mind that all this paper gets covered with paint.

1 large sheet of text paper, 19 x 25 inches (48.3 x 63.5 cm), or leftovers from other projects (it's fun to use a mixture of different papers)

Weights (page 18)

Painting, drawing, and collage supplies, such as acrylic paint, watercolor crayons, acrylic ink, graphite stick, paintbrushes (see Creative Techniques, page 28)

Sandpaper: 220 grit

Polycrylic Protective Finish (satin) and paintbrush

Corner rounder (page 14; optional)

Small scraps of decorative paper for embellishment

Hole punches: traditional, craft, and/or Japanese versions (page 14; optional)

Binder clip

Sewing machine

Straight pin

4. Once the glue is dry, put it under weights for at least an hour.

5. Have fun making a colorful surface using acrylic paints, watercolor crayons, graphite, and acrylic ink. As far as the overall design goes, keep in mind that you will be cutting this sheet down to make small covers. If you're not happy with what you have, add more paint and keep working on it.

6. Once you have covered both sides with paint and the paper has had a chance to dry, you can use fine sandpaper to sand all or parts of the paper. This allows lower layers of color to come through.

7. Brush Polycrylic over each side. This adds a protective layer and also strengthens the paper. Once the Polycrylic is dry, lightly sand again to remove any shine.

8. Decide on the dimensions of your notebook. Mine measures 6 x 3 ½ inches (15.2 x 8.9 cm). Cut out a piece of your "new" repurposed surface paper and trim it to your notebook's dimensions. The cover is one piece folded in half, so I doubled the width. My final cover measurement is 12 x 3 ½ inches (30.5 x 8.9 cm).

9. Round the corners, if desired.

10. Embellish the cover as desired with collage, acrylic ink, markers, and hole punches.

11. Measure and find the center fold line of your cover. Because the paper is thick, you will need to score the fold line before folding. Place a metal ruler along the fold line and draw your fettling knife along the line. Do not push down hard or you will cut the paper as you pull your knife along the ruler.

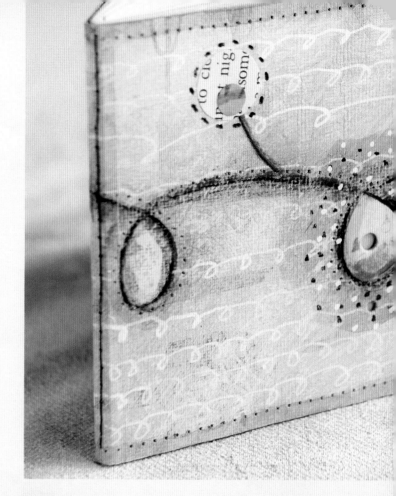

12. Make two more score lines ⅛ inch (3 mm) to either side of the center fold line. This gives you an allowance so the notebook will fold flat once you sew in the signature.

13. Gently fold along all three lines and set the folds using a bone folder.

14. The text block for this book contains only one signature consisting of five sheets. Using a craft knife and metal ruler, cut five sheets of text paper the same height as your cover and ¼ inch (6 mm) less than the width; mine measure 11¾ x 3½ inches (29.8 x 8.9 cm).

15. Fold the sheets in half and trim the fore edges (page 15) to clean them up.

16. Round the corners of the signature if you'd like. If your cover is rounded but your signature is not, your paper dimensions need to be ⅛ inch (3 mm) smaller all around so that the corners will not stick out past the cover.

17. Place the signature inside the open cover. Use a binder clip at the center fold line to hold it all in place while sewing. **C**

C

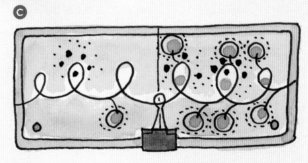

18. With the cover facing up, machine-sew along the center line using a basting stitch (6 to 7 stitches per inch [2.5 cm]), removing the binder clip when about an inch (2.5 cm) away. Sew slowly to make sure that you are following that center line. Leave the sewing thread at least 4 inches (10.2 cm) long on each side.

19. To tie off the thread ends, open the notebook to the center. At one end, gently pull up the inside thread. This will pull a loop of the outside thread to the inside. Use a straight pin to pull the loop though so that you have both thread ends on the inside. **D** Tie a square knot (page 24, figure B) as far to the inside as possible. Trim the ends to ¼ inch (6 mm). Repeat at the other end. Sometimes I add just a tiny dab of glue to the knot to make sure it stays secure.

D

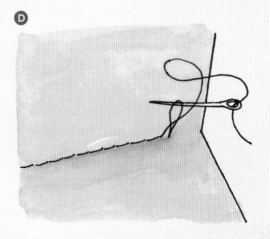

CLOTH BOOKS

Fabric makes a fun and unique cover for books. The sky's the limit for pattern and color. These covers are also a good way to use cloth scraps and repurpose old clothes you can't bear to pass on because you love the fabric and the memories attached to them. There's no glue involved here, only sewing. On the following pages are instructions for two versions: both are cloth, but one is soft and the other is more rigid. If you want to make the rigid version, skip ahead to page 69 for the modifications.

MAKE

1. Decide on the dimensions of your book; this can be dictated by the fabric you are using. For your first book I recommend making something no larger than 12 inches (30.5 cm) (when the book is closed) in any direction. Because these books have soft covers, smaller dimensions make for a more stable book. The one shown here and described in the following instructions is approximately 7 x 7½ inches (17.8 x 19 cm) when closed. For this size, you need an overall cover size of 15 x 7½ inches (38.1 x 19 cm). This is the dimension of the open cover with a 1-inch (2.5 cm) allowance for the spine (where the pages are sewn into the cover).

2. Pick a background fabric for the outside cover and tear (if using cotton fabric) or cut it to the size you want (remembering to double the width and add 1 inch [2.5 cm] for the spine). The torn edges create a raw but finished-looking edge. Pull off any loose threads.

3. Cut or tear shapes for the design on your outside cover and build the finished image. Remember that the full cover will be folded in half as a finished book. At this point you will have fabric shapes just sitting unattached on your cover. Carefully remove the shapes and set them aside in a way that maintains your layout. Ⓐ

4. Pick a fabric for the inside cover. Cut or tear it to the same size as the outside cover.

5. Tear or cut one to three layers of fabric (I used muslin) so that they are the same size, or slightly smaller, as the inside and outside covers to use as layers

GATHER

Basic Bookmaking Tool Kit (page 13)

3 sheets of Murano text paper, each 19 x 25 inches (48.3 x 63.5 cm)

Decorative or tissue paper, 11 x 14 inches (27.9 x 35.6 cm)

Scrap paper for a hole-punching template, a bit larger than your book cover (page 23)

½ yard (45.7 cm) of fabric, scraps, old clothing, old linens, or any fabric that excites you in colors and patterns that you want to combine; I use mostly cotton fabrics so that I can tear instead of cut the fabric.

½ yard (45.7 cm) of muslin or other cotton fabric to use for the inside layers of the cover

1 or 2 squares of felt in matching or contrasting colors for decoration (optional)

Iron and ironing board (optional)

Straight pins

Sewing machine (optional; this book can be made with hand-sewing)

Sewing needles: one for sewing thread, one for sewing embroidery floss

1 or 2 skeins of embroidery floss in contrasting colors for embellishment (optional)

2 or 3 colors of contrasting and/or matching sewing thread

Old phone book

1 yard (91.4 cm) of 3- or 4-ply linen thread, waxed or unwaxed

Binding needle (page 16)

Button for closure (optional)

between the covers. This gives the book stability while still maintaining the feel of a soft book. The number of layers depends on the weight of the fabric used for your covers; heavier fabric covers need fewer interior layers.

6. Iron your fabric and shapes, if needed.

7. Place the interior layers between the inside and outside covers and pin them in place. Machine- or hand-sew the layers together. (If you are using a machine, set the stitch length to 6 or 7 stitches per inch [2.5 cm] so the layers don't pucker). This can be done in a horizontal, vertical, or random pattern while making sure that you have sewn within ¾ to 1 inch (1.9 to 2.5 cm) from the outside edges of the cover (so the layers will not flap). You can also sew straight or zigzag stitches along the raw edges, if desired.

8. Arrange the shapes back onto the outside cover and attach by hand- or machine-sewing. I like to use a combination of the two and add some hand-sewn details as well. **B**

9. For the text block, measure the cover to figure out the size of the sheets. The sheet is the size of the open cover minus 1¼ inches (3.2 cm) horizontally and ½ inch (1.3 cm) vertically. In the example here, where the open cover is 15 x 7½ inches (38.1 x 19 cm), the sheet dimensions are 13¾ x 7 inches (34.9 x 17.8 cm). Tear text paper to these page dimensions for the interior of your book. The book shown here has three signatures of four sheets each (so 12 sheets of paper).

10. Put your signatures of text paper together and fold them in half. Use a bone folder to set the folds.

11. Tear the decorative paper or tissue paper for end sheets and end caps for the signatures. End sheets wrap around each signature and are like an extra page on top of your signature. They are sized slightly smaller than the text pages for the first and last signatures. End caps extend only 2 inches (5.1 cm) on either side of the text page. Sizing can be tailored to your liking.

12. Make the template for punching holes in your signature with scrap paper. Cut a piece of scrap paper 4 inches (10.2 cm) wide by the height of your text paper.

For the one shown here, I cut a piece of paper 4 x 7 inches (10.2 x 17.8 cm). Fold it in half vertically and mark places for the holes in the center of the fold. The holes should be ½ inch (1.3 cm) from the top and bottom, and evenly spaced no more than 3 inches (7.6 cm) apart (see Making a Template, page 23); my book has five holes.

13. Using the template, punch holes in each four-sheet signature with a needle tool, an awl, or an extra-large needle. Place the template in the fold of each signature and line up the top and bottom edges. (I use an open phone book to cradle the template and signature.) Hold the pages and template securely and punch the holes. **C**

14. Fold the cover in half and mark the inside center of the cover with a straight pin. Open the cover and lay it flat. Place the open middle signature along the fold line (marked with a pin) of the open cover. Insert the needle tool into the center hole of the middle signature and through the cover. Leave the awl in the hole. Use another needle tool, awl, or needle to punch the next hole. Leave that tool in place and use a third tool to punch the next hole. **D** This allows you to punch

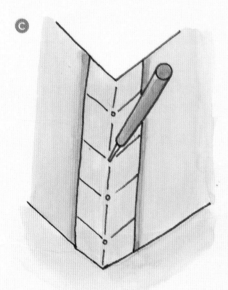

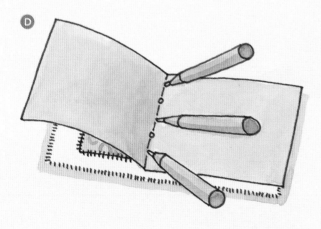

the holes while the signature and cover are held in place. Continue to punch all holes through the cover. Remember to remove the straight pin from the center fold before sewing.

15. Bind the book using the five-hole pamphlet stitch (page 25). Thread 1 yard (91.4 cm) of linen thread onto a binding needle. Sew the middle signature to the cover. Start sewing at the center hole from the inside of the signature, leaving a 3-inch (7.6 cm) tail of thread. Come out of the hole directly above the center hole and enter the next hole to the left. Then sew back down, in and out, and continue to the right until you are back up to the center hole. You will be sewing in a figure-eight pattern. Tie off the thread with a square knot (page 24, figure B). Trim the ends to ¼ inch (6 mm).

16. Repeat the sewing with the first and third signatures, placing them ¼ inch (6 mm) on either side of the middle signature so that you end up with three parallel lines of stitching for the binding.

17. I used a couple optional finishings for this book.

POCKET: Cut or tear a rectangle of fabric for a pocket on the inside front cover. Fold the rectangle in half, wrong sides together. Use a zigzag stitch on the sewing machine to finish the edges. Hand-sew the pocket to the inside cover. **E**

TIE CLOSURE: Tear two strips of fabric and sew them onto the front and back edge of the cover. Tie in a bow to close. **G**

E

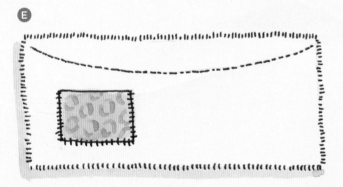

F

 **STIFF-COVER BOOK**

These covers have the look of a cloth-cover book, but use fusible interfacing to create a more rigid cover—the finished quality has the feel of canvas and is very sturdy. Try the button tie closure for an alternative decorative clasp.

GATHER

Supplies listed on page 65

½ yard (45.7 cm) of fusible horsehair canvas or mid- to heavyweight fusible interfacing

MAKE

1. Follow step 1 on page 65.

2. When you reach step 2, cut a piece of fusible horsehair canvas or interfacing the size of your outside cover dimensions minus ¼ inch (6 mm) on each side. Then follow the manufacturer's instructions for fusing the canvas or interfacing to the back side of your fabric. You can repeat this process with your inside cover fabric if you want an even more rigid book.

NOTE: If you use two layers of horsehair canvas or interfacing you only need one or two layers of fabric in the middle of your covers.

3. Continue with steps 3–17.

4. Sew a button to the front cover on the right-hand edge. Sew a strip of torn fabric (6 to 8 inches [15.2 to 20.3 cm] long) to the back cover, matching the placement of the button on the front. This strip wraps around the button to make a closure for your book.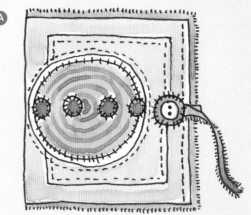

What is a book? Defining what a book is in the beginning of the twenty-first century is not an easy task. It's similar to the Indian fable asking six blind men to describe an elephant. Each differs in his description, claiming the beast to be smooth, tall, thin, round, sharp, and wide—its nature is recounted in its parts rather than as a whole. Herein lies the difficulty with reducing the definition of a book to one concept: it's many things to many people and cultures.

I can't account for other people's descriptions about a book, but for me it's a codex, a scroll, a concertina fold, a multidimensional, sided entity that opens in numerous ways, not just from the right but also from the left, or even from the top. It can be held in the palm of your hand, unravel, cascade down steps, or hang on a wall or even a clothesline. Until the advent of the computer, the book was, in Western culture, a finite printed object with a sequence of words, passages, and pages the reader turned from beginning to end. In a digital age, the influence of various software programs on the structure of the book has exploded along with the fertile content of ideas, placement, and layering of images on a page. The interactive nature of the computer, as an idea, when physically applied to the codex alters how it functions as a singular and narrative read. By writing in the margins or over existing images and text, drilling out the printed word, and adding ephemera such as paint, photography, and objects, for example, the book as a container of the author's original intent becomes a collaboration with an artist's interventions.

Disconnecting Old Glory, Doug Beube
PHOTOGRAPH BY DOUG BEUBE

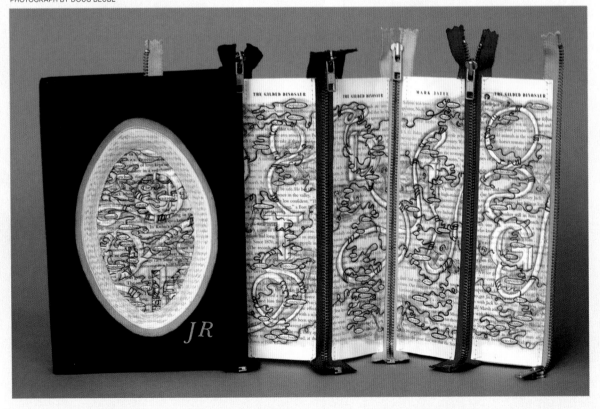

What is Radical Bookworks? In the mid-1980s I began teaching courses in altering found books. The full title, Radical Bookworks: From Meaning to Structure, was an appropriate response to the plethora of inexpensive used books in secondhand bookstores, flea markets, recycling centers, and the trash. With the emergence of the computer, the codex seemed to become obsolete, supplanting it with e-books and reading them from an electronic device. Books didn't vanish, and I suspect they never will. However, the codex and publishing are like an endangered species; they are diminishing. With billions of existing books in the world, raw materials are readily available for artists appropriating them and altering their structure, overlaying their content, and turning them into sculpture and installation.

I use the term Radical Bookworks to refer to challenging common assumptions about the nature of the book; it incorporates collage, installation, mixed media, painting, photography, sculpture, and writing. By exploring a variety of alternative structures, the physical properties of a book, and sequential relationships between both paginated works that include imagery and text and three-dimensional objects, the book becomes a heuristic tool, teaching viewers how to read it as they turn pages. When a book becomes radicalized, it functions as a sequence of complex ideas that employs found and unusual materials. Three-dimensional book objects that integrate alternative binding structures into meaningful artworks editorializes the viewpoint of the artist, whether it is personal, social, or political.

Why do you work in books? The codex has a long and esteemed history filled with references to art, culture, and and politics. One of its functions is to perpetuate both information and knowledge within culture. With the advent of the digital age, the book is becoming inconsequential, an outdated technology in which to store information compared to the massive ability of a computer. Books are readily available, inexpensive, rich with

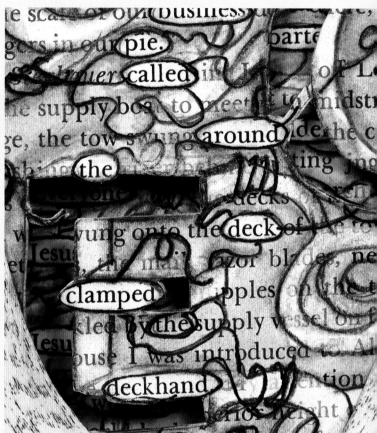

Disconnecting Old Glory (detail), Doug Beube
PHOTOGRAPH BY DOUG BEUBE

content, and charged with significance. When I select a book for a specific piece, choosing the title, paper quality, images, thickness, or number of pages are some of my considerations for working with an existing author's text or imagery. The book can be one-of-a-kind or assimilated into an installation that utilizes other media. The bookwork is the spine of other mediums; it's a synthesis of a physical form that can be appropriated, attacked, supported, carved out, or left as is. Bookworks are in the tradition of Marcel Duchamp's "ready-mades." They are altered to a degree but still maintain their recognition as functional and purposeful objects.

ZIPPITY-DO-DA BOOK

Here's a fabric-covered book that's both soft and rigid at the same time. It's quick and easy to put together, and like the Cloth Books (page 64), it can utilize fabric scraps or old clothing. This project would be a great kids' activity, too. Instead of using the sewing machine, mark the stitching lines and have them hand-sew around the boards.

MAKE

1. Decide on the dimensions for your book. Cut the board for the covers, rounding the corners if desired. For the book shown here, my boards are 5 x 7 inches (12.7 x 17.8 cm).

2. Make a paper pattern from your dimensions, adding 1 inch (2.5 cm) all around and $1/2$ inch (1.3 cm) for the spine. For mine, the width is 12 $1/2$ inches (31.8 cm) (1 + 5 + $1/2$ + 5 + 1 inch), and the length is 9 inches (22.9 cm) (1 + 7 + 1). That means my final measurements for the pattern are 12 $1/2$ x 9 inches (31.8 x 22.9 cm).

3. Pin the pattern to the knit fabric and cut it out. Repeat so that you have two pieces of fabric.

4. Sew on the fabric shapes for the surface design, if desired, using a ball-point needle in your machine. You can also add things after the book is finished, but it's much easier to do it at this stage.

5. Lay one piece of fabric face down. Use a glue stick to put a very small amount of glue in the center of each board. This will hold the fabric in place while you are positioning everything. Place the boards down on the cover, making sure there is $1/2$ inch (1.3 cm) between the boards and 1 inch (2.5 cm) all around the outside edge.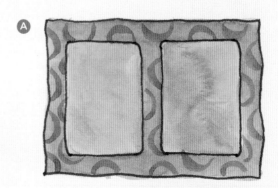

6. Place a small amount of glue on top of each board. Place the second fabric cover face up on top of the bottom cover and boards. Pin it in place.

7. Sew around the outside edge of the boards. The zipper presser foot allows stitching right up against the boards. Be sure to backstitch or tie off the ends of the thread.

8. Sew along both inside edges, creating the spine of the book. Again, backstitch or tie off the ends of the thread.

GATHER

Basic Bookmaking Tool Kit (page 13)

Shirt board or thin binder's board, 8 x 10 inches (20.3 x 25.4 cm)

15 sheets of text paper, each 8$1/2$ x 11 inches (21.6 x 28 cm)

Scrap paper for making a pattern, about 13 x 9 inches (33 x 22.9 cm)

Scrap paper for making a hole-punching template (page 23)

Corner rounder (page 14; optional)

Straight pins

$1/3$ yard (30.5 cm) of knit fabric

Fabric scraps for surface design

Sewing machine

Ball-point needle (for stretch fabric)

Sewing thread

Zipper presser foot for sewing machine

Old phone book

Erasable sewing marker or chalk

1 yard (91.4 cm) of linen thread

Binding needle

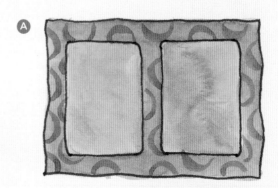

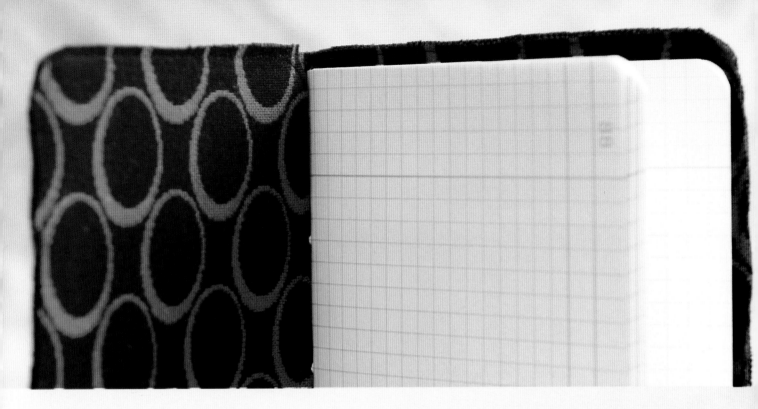

9. Trim the excess fabric a little more than ⅛ inch (3 mm) from the stitching. Because the fabric is knit, it won't unravel. Ⓑ

10. For the text block, cut and fold text paper for one multisheet signature. I used about 15 sheets cut to 8½ x 11 inches (21.6 x 28 cm).

11. Make a template for the sewing stations of a five-hole pamphlet stitch (page 23).

12. Punch holes in your signature (or signatures) with the needle tool. Place the template in the fold of the nested pages and line up the top and bottom edges. (I use an open phone book to cradle the template and signature.) Hold the pages and template securely and punch five holes with the needle tool.

13. Mark the sewing stations on the fabric spine with the template and a sewing marker or piece of chalk.

14. Bind the book with a five-hole pamphlet stitch (page 25) using linen thread and a binding needle.

NOTE: Because you used a dab of glue to hold the fabric in place while sewing the cover, the fabric may not lie completely flat and smooth. If this is the case, you can pull gently on the fabric in the middle of the cover and release the glue from the board.

Ⓑ

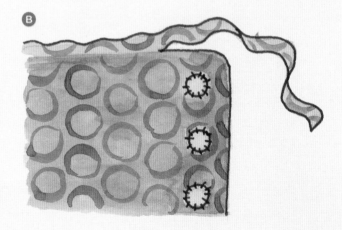

BOOK-BOARD COVERS

Book board, or Davey board, is usually covered with paper or book cloth when making book covers, but here's a variation on that old standard. I painted the boards using acrylic paint, then sanded some off to reveal layers underneath. The beauty of this technique is that if you don't like what you've painted, you can paint right over it and start again. Finishing it off with neutral-tone shoe polish or Johnson Paste Wax gives it a hand-rubbed look and creates a cover that's so much more than the sum of its parts.

GATHER

Basic Bookmaking Tool Kit (page 13)

Book board: midweight, 12 x 12 inches (30.5 x 30.5 cm)

12 sheets of text paper, 11 x 14 inches (28 x 35.6 cm)

Decorative paper for end sheets, 11 x 14 inches (28 x 35.6 cm)

Scrap paper for hole-making template (page 23)

Book cloth, commercial or handmade, 5 x 8 inches (12.7 x 20.3 cm)

Acrylic paint or milk paint

Paintbrushes

Sandpaper: 180 grit

Dust mask or respirator

Drawing, painting, and/or collage supplies (see Creative Techniques, page 28)

Spray fixative (optional)

Neutral shoe polish or Johnson Paste Wax

Cotton rag

Weights (page 18)

Old phone book

Binding needle

Linen thread

MAKE

1. Decide on the dimensions of your book. The one shown is 6 x 6 inches (15.2 x 15.2 cm). Cut two pieces of board to this size using a craft knife and ruler. You do not need to worry about grain direction in this project.

2. Using acrylic paint or milk paint, coat both sides of each board. You can paint as many layers as you want, but you must repeat the same number of layers on each side of the board; this keeps the board from warping. If you are creating a design or an image on the front and back, you won't need to repeat this layer on the other side unless the painted design is very thick or you notice that the board is warping. For the boards to stay flat, the moisture content on each side must be equal. Make sure that you paint the edges of your board as well because they will show.

3. Sand the painted boards until they have the texture you like. If this step feels too open-ended, experiment on a scrap piece of painted board until you get the hang of it. If you sand off too much paint, you can recoat the board. It's actually hard to make a mistake here that you can't fix! Be sure to wear a dust mask or respirator when sanding paint.

4. Draw, collage, or paint some more for any surface design you don't want sanded.

5. Spray the covers with fixative to set the surface. Or you can rub on shoe polish or paste wax with a cotton rag and burnish. This seals the surface and adds a layer of protection from dirt and moisture.

6. Decide on the number of signatures you want. This will affect the dimensions of the spine—the larger the number of signatures, the wider the spine. Generally, you need to allow 1/4 inch (6 mm) for each signature plus at least 2 inches (5.1 cm) for overlap (1 inch on each side). My book has three signatures, so my spine strip width is 2 3/4 inches (7 cm) (3/4 inch for the three signatures + 2 inches for overlap). The height of my book is 6 inches (15.2 cm), so the overall dimensions I need are 2 3/4 x 6 inches (7 x 15.2 cm).

7. The spine is made from two strips of book cloth that are glued together back to back. Use the measurements from step 6 to cut two book cloth strips. Using book glue, glue them together back to back.

8. On the inside of each cover, lightly sand 1 inch (2.5 cm) on each spine edge where the book cloth and board will overlap. This is to make sure that the shoe polish or wax won't inhibit the glue from making a solid bond between the painted board and the book cloth.

9. On the outside of your book cloth strip, use a pencil and ruler to draw a line—as lightly as possible—defining the spine in the center of your strip. This lets you see where to place the boards when gluing. The cloth strip is going to be glued to the inside of your covers with the spine strip showing.

10. Carefully brush glue along one side of the pencil line and out to the side. Place one cover face up on the strip. Gently use your bone folder to remove air bubbles, being careful to wipe up any excess glue. Repeat for the other cover.

NOTE: It's easy to get mixed up here and glue your covers in the wrong direction. Use a small sticky note to mark the front, back, and inside of the covers and save yourself some frustration!

11. Lay your cover open flat and put it under weights for at least one hour.

12. Find the dimensions of the paper needed for your signatures and cut or tear paper for the text block. My book is 6 x 6 inches (15.2 x 15.2 cm), so each sheet needs to be 11¾ x 5⅞ inches (29.8 cm). If your book's size is different, just subtract ¼ inch (6 mm) from the width of two pages and ⅛ inch (3 mm) from the book's length. I have four sheets to a signature and three signatures, so I cut 12 sheets of text paper. At this point you can also cut or tear end sheets from decorative paper for each signature if you'd like. End sheets wrap around each signature and are like an extra page on top of your signature (page 18). They are sized slightly smaller than the text pages for the first and last signatures. The middle signature end sheet extends only 2 inches (5.1 cm) on either side of the text page. Sizing can be tailored to your liking.

13. Make template for a five-hole pamphlet stitch (see Making a Template, page 23).

14. Punch holes in your signatures with the needle tool. Place the template in the fold of each signature and line up the top and bottom edges. (I use an open phone book to cradle the template and signature.) Hold the pages and template securely and punch five holes with the needle tool.

15. With your cover lying open flat on top of a closed phone book, use your template to mark where the holes need to be punched. If you have three signatures you need to space the lines of holes evenly apart. The easiest way to do this is to mark the exact middle of the spine and punch those holes. Then move ¼ inch (6 mm) to the left and mark the other holes; repeat ¼ inch (6 mm) to the right of the first line of holes for the third signature. Ⓐ

16. Sew the signatures to the spine with a five-hole pamphlet stitch (page 25), using the binding needle and linen thread.

 # A DIFFERENT SPINE

These covers lend themselves to several different binding styles. The primary instructions for the project use the pamphlet stitch, but the Coptic stitch (page 26) works well, too. For yet another variation on the spine, two pieces of board can be glued together with the book-cloth spine sandwiched between them; you end up with the spine ends hidden, and it gives a very finished look to the cover. Want to make it? Read on!

GATHER

Supplies listed on page 76

Thin board, 24 x 24 inches (61 x 61 cm) (Homemade Book Board, page 17, works well here)

MAKE

1. Cut the board into four 5 x 7-inch (12.7 x 17.8 cm) rectangles. Label the boards 1A, 1B, 2A, and 2B.

2. Follow the instructions as on page 76 except that you will be painting all four boards in step 2. There doesn't need to be much attention to what is painted on the inside of each board, only that it gets the same number of coats of paint as the outside. Only sand and wax the outside of each board, not the inside.

3. Continue as before with preparing a book cloth strip (steps 7–11). To make sure that your book cloth strip will fit seamlessly between the two layers of board, you need to remove a thin layer of board to allow for the thickness of the book cloth. Measure in 1 inch (2.5 cm) from the spine edge on the inside of board 1B. Using a craft knife, lightly cut along this 1-inch (2.5 cm) line. Be careful not to cut all the way through the board. Because the book board is made of layers of paper you will be able to peel back a few layers along this strip. 🅐🅑

4. Because the back and front cover are now made up of two boards each, the gluing sequence is a bit different. First glue the book-cloth strip along the spine line (the area you have peeled) to the inside of board 1B. Use the bone folder to remove air bubbles. Brush glue

on the inside of board 1A. Wipe away any glue on the edge of the board. Match boards 1A and 1B together. Press firmly on the boards. Glue boards 2A and 2B the same way, starting with the cloth strip. Put the open, flat glued covers under a weight for at least one hour.

5. Bind as in steps 13–16.

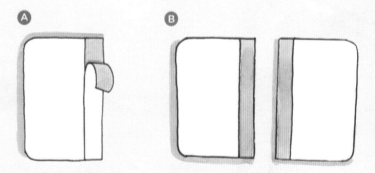

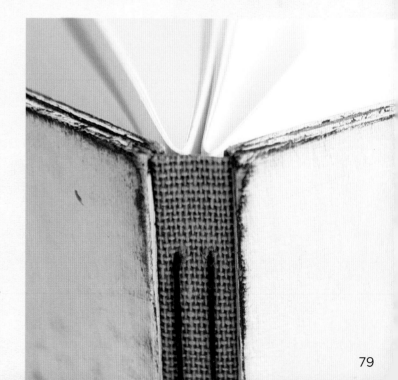

TRAVEL COMPANION

This is a refined yet practical version of your typical blank book. The cover is made from sturdy, flexible paper that wraps around the fore edge of the book to help keep everything inside while also allowing for expanding "innards" (all the bits and pieces you collect).

MAKE

NOTE: You don't need to worry about the paper grain in this project.

1. Decide on the dimensions for your journal. Take into account what size and shape will give you ease of use while traveling. Also decide on the number and type of signatures you want to make (blank, drawing, pocket) and the length of the wrap. I chose to make a 5 x 7-inch (12.7 x 17.8 cm) journal with a 3-inch (7.6 cm) wrap.

2. Because the cover is made from a single piece of paper, you need to plan it all out from the start. Start by making a dummy of your cover with scrap paper. This allows you to play around with the spine width and the overall visuals of your cover before cutting your good paper. For the spine width, count the number of signatures. Blank signatures need about ⅛ inch (3 mm) on either side; drawing and pocket page signatures need ¼ inch (6 mm) on either side. My 5 x 7-inch (12.7 x 17.8 cm) journal needed a spine width of 1⅜ inches (3.5 cm) (three signatures of blank text paper at ⅛ inch [3 mm] each, and four pocket or drawing signatures at ¼ inch [6 mm] each). To this I added 3 inches (7.6 cm) for the wrap. So my final cover measurement was 14⅜ x 7 inches (36.6 x 17.8 cm) (5 + 1⅜ + 5 + 3 inches x 7 inches).

3. Cut or tear cover paper to your dummy measurements.

4. Place the cover paper face down on your self-healing cutting mat.

5. Measure and mark the spine width you calculated in step 2 (mine was 1⅜ inches [3.5 cm]) with a pencil.

6. Place your ruler along one spine edge. Score gently with a fettling knife. Repeat on the other edge.

7. Fold along the spine edges. Use a bone folder to set the fold so you have a nice, clean edge. Because the paper is heavy, it should hold the shape of the spine.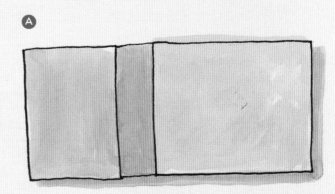

8. Cut or tear paper for the cover pocket. Mine was about 4 x 3 inches (10.2 x 7.6 cm).

GATHER

Basic Bookmaking Tool Kit (page 13)

Heavy, strong paper for the cover, 8 x 20 inches (20.3 x 50.8 cm): This needs to be a paper that is flexible; a handmade paper with strong fiber content works well.

6 sheets of text paper, each 19 x 25 inches (48.3 x 63.5 cm): This should be a combination of paper for journaling, drawing paper (Rives BFK), and a midweight paper (Murano) for pocket pages.

Scrap paper: for the dummy cover, 8 x 20 inches (20.3 x 50.8 cm), and for the hole-making template (page 23)

3 yards (2.7 m) of linen thread

Masking tape (optional)

Threaded sewing machine or needle and thread

Old phone book

Binding needle

Fabric strip for cover closure

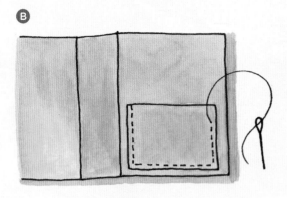

9. Position the pocket on the front right side of the cover between the fore edge and the right-hand score line. Using a running stitch, sew the pocket on with linen thread. You can use masking tape to hold the pocket down in a few places as you sew. Just make sure the tape won't damage your cover by testing it first. **B** If the thick cover paper is hard to sew through, prepunch the holes with the needle and then sew.

10. Cut or tear paper for the text block. In this journal my signatures are the same height as my cover (7 inches [17.8 cm]) and twice the width minus ¼ inch (6 mm) (9¾ inches [24.8 cm]). For pocket signatures, cut or tear your paper to the same dimensions as a regular signature with 3 inches (7.6 cm) added to the height (so mine would be 9¾ x 10 inches [24.8 x 25.4 cm]). Using a ruler, score and fold the paper 3 inches (7.6 cm) from the bottom. Machine- or hand-sew the fold down on either side, ¼ inch (6 mm) in from the edge. If you're using a machine, set your stitch length to 6 or 7 stitches per inch (2.5 cm) (basting stitch). Tie off or knot the threads at the ends. **C** I used two pocket pages back to back to make one signature.

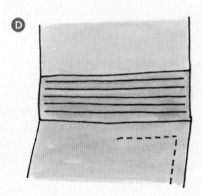

11. The book is bound with a five-hole pamphlet stitch (page 25). Make a template for the sewing stations (page 23).

12. One at a time, place your signatures in the middle of an open phone book and punch the sewing stations using your template and a needle tool.

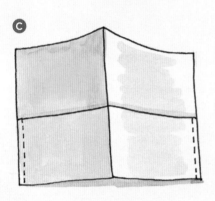

13. With your cover face down and using a ruler, measure and mark the signatures' sewing lines on the inside of the spine with a pencil. **D** My book has seven signatures, so I will need seven sewing lines. I space these according to the allowances made in step 2: ⅛ inch (3 mm) for each of the three blank text-paper signatures, and ¼ inch (6 mm) each for the four drawing and pocket signatures. Come in ⅛ inch (3 mm) from the spine edge on either side. Moving left to right from the left spine edge, my sewing lines are ⅛ inch (3 mm), ¼ inch (6 mm), ¼ inch (6 mm), ¼ inch (6 mm), ¼ inch (6 mm), ⅛ inch (3 mm), and ⅛ inch (3 mm) apart.

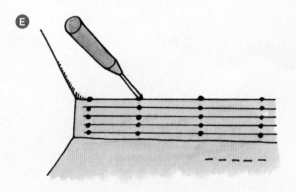

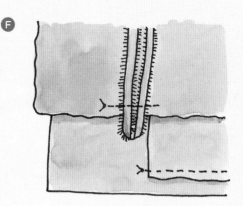

14. Place your cover face down on a closed phone book. Fold your template in half lengthwise, and line up the folded edge with each sewing line. Using a needle tool, punch each sewing station along the sewing line. You will be punching five holes along each line. Be careful to correctly line up your template so that sewing lines will be straight and parallel. **E**

15. Bind the book with a five-hole pamphlet stitch (page 25) using linen thread and a binding needle.

16. I like my Travel Companions to have a closure to keep all the goodies inside as I travel. To make one, tear a 1/2-inch (1.3 cm) strip of fabric twice the width of the cover (so 15 3/8 inches x 2 = 31 inches [78.7 cm] for mine).

17. Fold the strip in half crosswise. Extend the loop of the fold over the end of the cover by 1/2 inch (1.3 cm). With linen thread, use a running stitch up and then down to sew it in place. **F**

NOTE: The text block of this book contains signatures of blank paper for writing; signatures of good drawing paper for drawings, collages, or watercolors; and signatures of pocket pages where you can slip in all the various items you pick up. The beauty of this journal is that it can be customized to suit your preferences—whether you want more blank writing pages, no drawing paper, or all pocket pages. The five-hole pamphlet stitch is sturdy and easily accommodates any combination or variation of signatures. It's also easy to take apart in case you want to include some of the actual pages of this journal into a Travel Journal (page 94).

When I take a big trip I like to carry a blank book like this one along to record events and sights. Invariably, I also pick up bits and pieces of brochures, ticket stubs, and fun papers along the way—oh, yes, and the inevitable candy wrappers from newly discovered taste treats! These get stuffed into the book in a haphazard manner waiting to be organized once I return home. When the dust has settled, the bags are unpacked, and I'm back in my studio routine, I spend time making a book (like the Travel Journal on page 94) to contain these musings, papers, and any photos I took during the trip. By combining all these elements into one book it becomes much more than a record of the trip—it becomes more like a story. Life goes on, and details fade, but no matter how much time passes, when I sit down and open this book, the essence of the trip is there between the pages.

Have you always made books? No, but one has been in my hand almost as long as I can remember. The first book I read was *Austin Boys—Adrift*. I can still recall the red cover. The spine cover was torn, so I would examine how the book was put together.

Having grown up around farmers, I was in fact happy not to make a book from scratch. Books came from elsewhere, ready-made, and they were like messengers from the larger world. I liked not having to make them. The irony is that now I realize I am drawn to making books so that I experience the physical act of creation again, like I did working with my hands as a young person in the field.

What do you love about books? They are compact, physical, a world between two covers. I can go anywhere when I'm reading. And now I can make books and create new worlds, enhancing the words of an author or a poet with handmade paper and a binding. With good choices, I can extend the world of the author outward to the very moment a reader first touches and sees the book.

Can you talk about traditional and nontraditional bookbinding? I suggest we first agree to consider the Western codex book form as our "traditional" and any other non-codex book made in a Western culture as "nontraditional." I consider, then, a traditional binding as being like a beautiful, simple machine. Making that machine work well, meaning good selection of sewing thread, spine width, thickness of the book boards, and so on, is an amazing challenge for each book, and a source of great satisfaction for me. The work is essentially me asking myself how I can respond to the words of the author with the binding as well as create a practical, long-lived structure.

Eye Think About Potatoes: They Make Me Quite Round, Frank Brannon
PHOTOGRAPH BY STEVE MANN

And now in the early twenty-first century, I feel we're in the midst of seeing nontraditional bookbindings enhance authors' words in new and exciting ways. What I imagine is that the book is freeing itself from a more pragmatic need, the need solely to communicate or record. Nontraditional bindings participate in that new exploration. In other words, we've had time since the European Industrial Revolution to redefine other fine crafts, such as pottery, glass, and metal, renegotiating form versus function. We know in these other disciplines that, sometimes, form now wins out. I think we're seeing book arts involved in this very renegotiation. And with these options a codex form might be the right approach to a particular project, and other times it is not. A contemporary book artist needs to consider a full set of options when approaching a new work.

How important is craftsmanship? In the paper mill of the University of Alabama's MFA in the Book Arts program, there is a quotation that hangs above the papermaking vat. The quotation is attributed to the twentieth-century papermaker Seikichiro Goto, and it says, "Even if a person doesn't make paper very skillfully, if he makes it honestly, it will be good paper. You can see it in the sheets. A craftsman must be honest from the spirit! If he avoids work or menial tasks, he's not sincere about papermaking." For me, this quotation is so clear in that right intention is a fundamental component of good craft. Along with intent, one learns the hand skills necessary to successfully create a book and its binding. This I feel is true for all book forms and their bindings.

And as an aside I note that there are so many good book artists of all genders that we need to develop a new word for craftsmanship.

Sentinels, 40 Panels of Handmade Mulberry Paper, Frank Brannon
PHOTOGRAPH BY STEVE MANN

POCKET BOOK

Most of us have letters and cards that we've saved over the years for one reason or another. Whether it's the actual words or the sentiments that they represent, these pieces of paper become dear to us. Often these keepsakes get stuffed into drawers or bound up and put away in boxes without easy access. The Pocket Book is a home for these letters and cards, so you can easily take them down from the shelf and revisit them anytime.

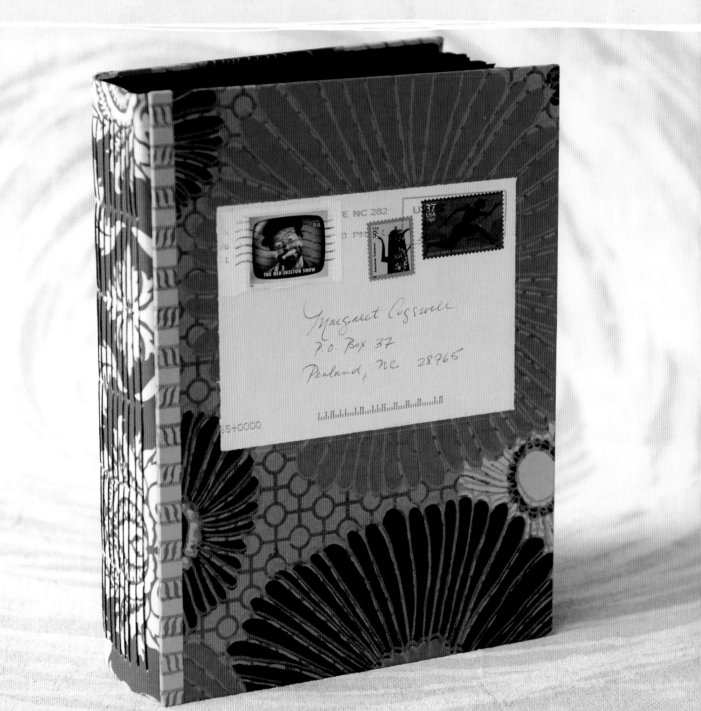

MAKE

NOTE: The signatures in this book are composed of single sheets because of the bulk associated with the pockets. Each sheet will yield four pocket pages.

1. Determine the dimensions for the book, keeping in mind the overall size of your cards and letters. Also think about how many signatures you want for your book. For the one shown here, I went with 7 1/2 x 10 inches (19 x 25.4 cm) and 10 signatures.

2. Cut two pieces of the midweight book board for the cover. Lightly sand the edges to take off any burrs.

3. On the back of each board, draw a line 1 inch (2.5 cm) in from the edge (whichever edge you choose will become the spine edge).

4. If you want to put a shallow recess on the front cover for a picture or title, use a pencil and ruler to mark off the recess. With a craft knife and metal ruler, cut down into the board about one-quarter of the way through. Use the point of your knife to dig up one of the corners and peel the layers away until you have a smooth and uniform surface. It's easier to peel the layers in the direction of the grain. Ⓐ

5. Precisely cut the decorative paper for the cover. For the outside paper, cut to your dimensions plus 1/2 inch (1.3 cm) all around. For the inside paper, cut to your dimensions minus 1/8 inch (3 mm) all around.

6. Determine the width of your spine. You need 1 inch (2.5 cm) for overlap on the front and back cover each, plus 1/4 inch (6 mm) for every signature. This spacing allows for the bulk of the cards and letters you will put in the book. For mine, I needed 4 1/2 inches (11.4 cm): 2 inches (5.1 cm) of overlap + 2 1/2 inches (6.4 cm) for 10 signatures.

GATHER

Basic Bookmaking Tool Kit
(page 13)

Book board: midweight,
20 x 24 inches (50.8 x 61 cm)

2 sheets of decorative paper for cover
(both inside and out), each 19 x 25
inches (48.3 x 63.5 cm)

15 sheets of heavy paper
(Murano) for pocket pages

Scrap paper for hole-making
template (page 23)

Book cloth for spine,
12 x 16 inches (30.5 x 40.6 cm)

Sandpaper: 100 grit

Weights (page 18)

Threaded sewing machine or needle
and thread

Old phone book

Linen thread

Binding needle

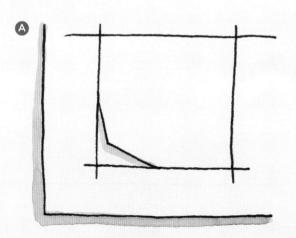

Ⓐ

B

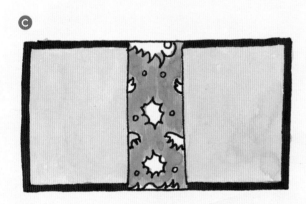

C

D

7. Cut two strips of book cloth—one the spine width by the height plus 4 inches (10.2 cm), and the other the spine width by the height minus 2 inches (5.1 cm). Because my spine width is 4½ inches (11.4 cm) and the height of my book is 10 inches (25.4 cm), my two strips are 4½ x 14 inches (11.4 x 35.6 cm) and 4½ x 8 inches (11.4 x 20.3 cm).

8. Using a pencil and ruler, draw a line on the back of the longer strip 1 inch (2.5 cm) down from the top and 1 inch (2.5 cm) up from the bottom. Brush book glue on the two 1-inch (2.5 cm) portions at the top and bottom.

9. Fold over the glued portions on the line you drew 1 inch (2.5 cm) from the top and bottom. Use a bone folder to smooth them out.

10. Brush book glue on the back of the shorter strip. Glue this to the back of the longer (folded) strip. The shorter strip should meet evenly with the end of the folded strip so that there is a smooth transition with no overlap.

11. Put these strips under a weight.

12. Glue the outside cover paper to the book boards.

13. Turn the boards over. On one board at a time, brush some glue inside the 1-inch (2.5 cm) portion you marked off in step 3. Line up the spine strip (created in steps 7–11) so that it overlaps along this 1-inch (2.5 cm) section. Repeat for the other board. Use the bone folder to make sure the cloth adheres to the board. **B**

14. Glue the inside cover paper to the boards. Note that 1 inch (2.5 cm) of your spine strip will be sandwiched between the back of the board and the inside cover paper. **C**

15. If you made a recess on the front cover in step 4, glue in a picture or title. **D** Put the whole cover under a weight for at least two hours.

16. Cut or tear the paper for your signatures. There will be only one sheet per signature. They should be twice the width of the book minus ¼ inch (6 mm) and the height of the book minus ⅛ inch (3 mm). My sheets are 14¾ x 9⅞ inches (37.5 x 25.1 cm), and I needed 10 of these. Fold each sheet in half.

17. Cut or tear the heavy paper for the pockets. These will be strips of the same paper as your signatures, but they should measure 6 inches (15.2 cm) wide by the length of your signature (in my case, 14¾ inches [37.5 cm]). Fold each pocket strip in half lengthwise.

18. Fit the folded pocket strips over the bottom of each signature. Use the bone folder to ease all folds now that there is bulk.

19. Using a sewing machine, sew the pocket strips to the signatures ¼ inch (6 mm) in from the edges, using a basting stitch (6 or 7 stitches per inch [2.5 cm]). Leave the thread ends long enough to tie off. Then tie off the threads using a square knot (page 24, figure B). Trim the remaining thread to ¼ inch (6 mm).

20. Because the pocket strips create bulk, spacers need to be added along the rest of the spine. Cut or tear 1-inch (2.5 cm) strips to the height of your signature minus 3 inches (7.6 cm). There will be two spacers for every signature (meaning one spacer on each side of the signature). Score each strip lengthwise in the middle using a fettling knife and ruler so they can be folded in half. Use the bone folder to set the fold. For my book with 10 signatures, I needed twenty 1-inch (2.5 cm) strips, folded in half lengthwise.

21. Make a template for a seven-hole pamphlet stitch (page 23). Cut a piece of scrap paper 4 inches (10.2 cm) wide by the length of your book. For the one shown here, I cut a piece of paper 4 x 10 inches (10.2 x 25.4 cm). Fold it in half vertically and mark places for the holes in the center of the fold. The holes should be ½ inch (1.3 cm) from each end and evenly spaced no more than 2 inches (5.1 cm) apart.

22. Working in an old phone book, line the fold of your template up with the fold of each signature. Punch sewing stations in the signatures and spacers with the needle tool.

23. Using a pencil and ruler, lightly mark off stitching lines every ¼ inch (6 mm) on the inside of the spine.

24. Using your template as a guide, punch sewing stations in the spine along each of the stitching lines.

25. Bind the book with the seven-hole pamphlet stitch (page 25) using linen thread and a binding needle (page 16). The spacers make the binding a bit challenging, so allow a little extra time.

MARGARET'S JOURNAL

The perfect journal for me is a 5 x 5-inch (12.7 x 12.7 cm) Coptic-stitch book filled with Hahnemühle Ingres paper. I want paper that is sturdy but not too heavy, and one that can handle drawing, collage, and water-based paints. Hahnemühle Ingres fits the bill. And for the binding, whatever your chosen size, the Coptic stitch (page 26) is a good choice for a journal because it allows every page to lie flat.

MAKE

1. Determine your dimensions. The journal shown here is 5 x 5 inches (12.7 x 12.7 cm).

2. Cut two pieces of book board to your dimensions. Sand the edges of the board to remove burrs, if necessary.

3. Mark and cut a recess in the front cover if desired (see step 4 of the Pocket Book, page 87).

4. Cut or tear decorative paper for the cover. For the outside paper, cut to your dimensions plus 1/4 inch (6 mm) on each side. For the inside, cut to your dimensions minus 1/8 inch (3 mm) on each side. For the one shown here, I cut two sheets to 5 1/2 x 5 1/2 inches 14 x 14 cm) for the outside, and two sheets to 4 3/4 x 4 3/4 inches (12 x 12 cm) for the inside.

5. One at a time, glue the boards to the cover paper with book glue. Follow the instructions for Making a Book Cover (page 22). Note that for this book you will also glue decorative paper on the inside of the covers. And, if you have a picture for your recess, now is also the time to glue the picture into the recess in the front cover using a glue stick. Make sure both boards sit under a weight for at least two hours.

6. Determine how many signatures you want. I have six signatures and four sheets to each signature.

NOTE: Coptic bindings need a minimum of four signatures for the book to be sturdy.

7. Cut or tear paper for your signatures. They should be twice the width of the book minus 1/4 inch (6 mm) and the height of the book minus 1/8 inch (3 mm). The one here is 9 3/4 x 4 7/8 inches (24.8 x 12.4 cm). Gather the pages into sets of four and fold in half to make each signature.

8. Make a template for the sewing stations for a Coptic binding (page 23). Cut a piece of scrap paper 4 inches (10.2 cm) wide by the length of your book. For the one

GATHER

Basic Bookmaking Tool Kit (page 13)

Book board: midweight, 8 x 12 inches (20.3 x 30.5 cm)

2 sheets of decorative paper for cover, 11 x 14 inches (27.9 x 35.6 cm)

4 sheets of Hahnemühle Ingres paper (100#), 19 x 25 inches (48.3 x 63.5 cm), or other quality paper

Scrap paper for hole-making template (page 23)

Sandpaper: 100 grit

Weights (page 18)

Old phone book

Linen thread

Bent or curved binding needle

shown here, I cut a piece of paper 4 x 5 inches (10.2 x 12.7 cm). Fold it in half vertically and mark places for the holes in the center of the fold. The first and last hole should be ½ inch (1.3 cm) from the top and bottom. The other holes are evenly spaced from 1 to 3 inches (2.5 to 7.6 cm) apart, depending on the height of your book and your preference. My book has five sewing stations: the outer two are ½ inch (1.3 cm) from the head and tail, and the other three are in between, 1 inch (2.5 cm) apart.

9. Put a signature into an open phone book and place your template in the middle of the signature. Using a needle tool, punch sewing stations in each signature.

10. To punch binding holes in the covers, lay the front cover face up on top of a closed phone book with the spine edge of the cover alongside the spine edge of the phone book. Fold your template in half so that the punching holes are visible along the folded edge. Place the template ¼ inch (6 mm) in from the spine edge of the cover and hold it in place with one hand. With your other hand, use the needle tool to mark each hole. Remove the template and fully punch each hole. You may need to turn the cover over and punch through from the back to make sure the hole is completely open. Repeat this process for the back cover. Ⓐ

11. Bind using the Coptic stitch (page 26).

Variation

THE OPTIONAL DISPLAY STAND

Because my journals are small and mostly images, I don't mind if others look through them—in fact, I often display them! Repurposed and found objects make excellent display stands, and they can even add to the overall experience of the journal. For this one, I found a wooden letter holder at the local thrift store. With some tinkering and milk paint, it soon had a new life!

GATHER

Wooden napkin holder or other similar object

Saw (optional)

Sandpaper, 100 and 150 grit

Acrylic paint

Paintbrushes

Scraps of book board

PVA glue

Johnson Paste Wax (optional)

Small drawer handle (optional)

MAKE

1. My original object had three partitions. I decided to saw two of the partitions off and make the back of the holder the front of my display stand. That way I could take advantage of the short cubbie in the back as well.

2. If you use wood, sand the whole thing with 100-grit sandpaper to take off the finish and distress it just a bit. You can use wood filler to smooth out the rough places left by anything you removed. Sand once more with 150-grit sandpaper to get it ready to paint.

3. I painted mine with two coats of acrylic paint.

4. Next I made a drawer for the cubbie out of scraps of book board and PVA glue. Several coats of acrylic paint, a finish coat of wax, and a small handle finished it off.

TRAVEL JOURNAL

Whether you use it as an old-fashioned photo album or a newfangled memory book, this is a great way to remember your travels. Combining text, photos, drawings, and papers from the trip with specially folded signatures bound with the Coptic stitch yields a keepsake that is both archival and full of life. The one shown here chronicles a walking trip to Scotland along the Great Glen Way, a 79-mile (126 km) trail from Fort William to Inverness along the Caledonian Canal. I took my written descriptions of each day's walk, edited them a bit, and rewrote them on translucent parchmentlike paper. I like the effect of this paper in front of a photo page; the interplay of the text and the photo creates its own unique image and adds to the experience of looking through the book. There are plenty of blank pages for mounting photos, and pocket pages at the back of the book can hold various items.

MAKE

1. Decide on the overall dimensions for the journal, keeping in mind the size of your photos and other items to be included. The one shown here is 10 x 7 inches (25.4 x 17.8 cm) with a 10 $\frac{1}{8}$ x 7 $\frac{1}{8}$-inch (25.7 x 18.1 cm) cover. If you make a different size, figure out your page size and then add $\frac{1}{8}$ inch (3 mm) to each measurement for the cover size.

2. Cut two pieces of book board to your cover size (10 $\frac{1}{8}$ x 7 $\frac{1}{8}$ inches [25.7 x 18.1 cm]). Sand the edges of the board with 100-grit sandpaper to remove any burrs, if necessary.

3. Mark and cut a recess in the front cover, if desired (see step 4 of the Pocket Book on page 87).

4. Cut or tear decorative paper for the cover. The paper for the outside should equal your cover dimensions plus $\frac{1}{4}$ inch (6 mm) all around (10 $\frac{5}{8}$ x 7 $\frac{5}{8}$ inches [26.3 x 18.7 cm]). The paper for the inside should measure your dimensions minus $\frac{1}{8}$ inch (3 mm) all around (10 x 7 inches [25.4 x 17.8 cm]).

5. One at a time, glue the boards to the cover paper with book glue. Follow the instructions for Making a Book Cover (page 22). Note that for this book you will also glue decorative paper on the inside of the covers. When you are finished with that, glue the title or a picture into the recess of the front cover with a glue stick. Make sure both boards sit under a weight for at least two hours.

6. Decide how many text pages, photo pages, and pocket pages you want. Here's how I figured it out for this book: This chronicled a seven-day walking trip, and I wanted the book to reflect the progression of the trip. I organized my photos by days and figured out how many photo pages I needed for each day. At this point, I wasn't sure how many pages I would need for the written portion (the text pages) each day, so I decided to go at it from a different direction. I knew I wanted to handwrite the text on the pages before I bound the book, so I estimated how many pages I would need and went ahead and wrote everything out. As I came to the end I was short a few pages, so I just cut more. For the pocket pages I looked at what I had to go inside of them; I figured I needed four pages. These, I decided, would be at the end of the book.

7. Cut or tear your pages. Add 1 inch (2.5 cm) to the width of each page for a spacer. For example, for my 10 x 7-inch (25.4 x 17.8 cm) book I made 11 x 7-inch (27.9 x 17.8 cm) pages. For each pocket page,

GATHER

Basic Bookmaking Tool Kit (page 13)

Book board, 20 x 24 inches (50.8 x 61 cm)

2 sheets of decorative paper, each 19 x 25 (48.3 x 63.5 cm)

12 sheets of cover-weight, acid-free black paper for photo and pocket pages, each 19 x 25 inches (48.3 x 63.5 cm)

12 sheets of translucent, acid-free paper for text pages, each 19 x 25 inches (48.3 x 63.5 cm)

Scrap paper for hole-making template (page 23)

Sandpaper: 100 grit

Weights (page 18)

Threaded sewing machine

Old phone book

Linen thread

Binding needle

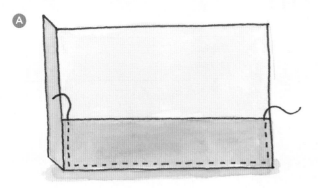

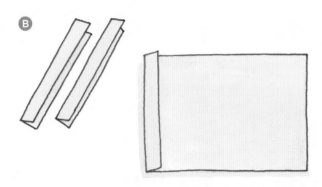

cut or tear an extra strip of 2½-inch (6.4 cm) black paper by your paper's width (so mine is 10 x 2½ inches [25.4 x 6.4 cm]).

8. Score and fold 1 inch (2.5 cm) in from the width of each page so you end up with a page of your original dimension (10 x 7 inches [25.4 x 17.8 cm]).

9. Sew the pocket pages (these can be glued or sewn by hand if you don't have a sewing machine). First align the 2½-inch (6.4 cm) strip along the bottom of your pocket page from the fold to the opposite edge. Sew it in place ¼ inch (6 mm) from the outside edge using a basting stitch with approximately 6 or 7 stitches per inch (2.5 cm). Ⓐ Tie off the ends of the thread with a square knot (page 24, figure B).

10. Decide whether you want a title page at the beginning and end caps for each signature. (An end cap is a narrow strip of decorative paper that covers the spine end of each signature. Its main function is decorative.) Ⓑ A title page has the same dimensions as a regular page. For end caps, cut a 2-inch (5.1 cm) strip the height of your page, and score and fold it vertically in the middle.

11. Arrange the photo and pocket pages into signatures. Because I used heavy paper, I have only two sheets per signature. The folded side is the spine edge. The pages are situated so that one fold is to the back and the next page's fold is to the front, creating a linked page equaling one signature. **C** These signatures want to spring apart, so I weight them as I am working. My text pages are on thin paper, so I just add them into the already assembled signatures of the heavy paper. This means you end up with signatures of different combinations and sequences of paper, depending on the photo and text sequence for the journal. **D**

12. If you have a title page, add it to the first signature; add optional end caps to follow the signatures.

13. Make a template for sewing stations in the text block and cover for a Coptic binding (page 23). Cut a piece of scrap paper 4 inches (10.2 cm) wide by the length of your book. For the one shown here, I cut a piece of paper 4 x 7 inches (10.2 x 17.8 cm). Fold it in half vertically and mark places for the holes in the center of the fold. My book has five sewing stations: two are ½ inch (1.3 cm) from the head and tail, and three are 1½ inches (3.8 cm) apart in between.

14. Lay the first signature in an open phone book and put the template on top, inside the fold and aligned with the top and bottom of the signature. Punch the sewing-station holes using a needle tool. Repeat for each signature as well as the title page and end caps, if using.

15. Bind your book with linen thread and a binding needle using the Coptic stitch (page 26). The spacer folds make this book a bit more difficult to bind than the average book. If you get frustrated, take a deep breath and hang in there. It will come together.

16. Now you are ready to add photos, drawings, and souvenir items to your pockets!

C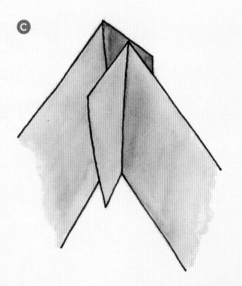

D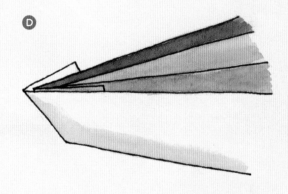

Translucent, photo, and pocket pages can be arranged in any order depending on how you want to organize your journal. Each of these pages is folded in a way that creates a spacer in the spine. This allows room for photos, drawings, and other items to be added to the book without the fore edge "yawning" (becoming wider than the spine). All the paper used to make the pages is archival, ensuring that this book lasts and maintains the quality of the photos and drawings over time.

UN-
CONVENTIONAL
BOOKS

UNBOUND BOOK

Who says a book has to be bound? A book can be made up of separate components that, when joined together, tell a story. Sometimes the sequence of the "pages" matters, but other times they are interchangeable, as in my story, "The Red-Crested Bellyacher."

MAKE

1. Thoroughly clean the container you plan to use. The surface might be just right without altering, but if you are going to paint or resurface it, it needs to be sanded to remove the old paint. If the existing surface is shiny, use fine sandpaper to dull the surface. Tin surfaces need to be scrubbed with a green scrubbie and dish detergent to remove any grease or oil residue.

2. If you have decided to decorate your container, now is the time to paint it. I used spray paint on my tin. First I applied a coat of primer, then several light coats of color.

3. Determine dimensions for your "pages" by measuring the circumference of your tin (or the perimeter of your container) and subtracting about 1/8 inch (3 mm).

4. Cut out about 10 pages (or however many you need to tell your story, as long as they will fit in your tin) from the Rives BFK paper.

GATHER

Basic Bookmaking Tool Kit (page 13)

1 sheet of Rives BFK paper, 25 x 36 inches (63.5 x 91.4 cm)

An old or found container of some sort, such as a shoe polish or candy tin or a wooden box

Sandpaper: 60, 150, and 220 grits

Green scrubbie (optional)

Liquid dishwasher detergent (optional)

Paint primer (optional)

Spray paint for tin; milk or acrylic paint for wood

Drawing, painting, and/or collage materials for illustrating the story and the cover (see Creative Techniques, page 28)

Paintbrushes

Spray fixative

Felt for lining your container

Beacon 527 Multi-Use Glue

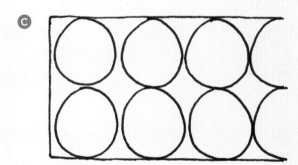

5. Illustrate your story on one side of each page. You can also add a small image on the back of each "page" to give it a finished look.

6. Apply spray fixative over your pages and let them dry.

7. Measure and cut felt for the inside top and bottom of your container. Glue the felt in place with Beacon 527 Multi-Use Glue.

8. Glue or paint a title on the cover.

9. Fill the completed container with your pages.

As a child, in my family, I was a carrottop amid a sea of blondes. I mean that kind of red hair that is impossibly red! To complete my charms, I was a squeaky wheel—better known as a whiner. Growing up in a family of four girls means one must speak up to be heard. My father had nicknames for each of his girls, but I had two: Doodlebug when I was cooperative (seldom) and the Red-Crested Bellyacher the rest of the time.

Recently one of my sisters gave me an empty shoe-polish tin. I figured it would make an excellent "cover" for "The Red-Crested Bellyacher," a story I created about that little mess of a girl I used to be. It just so happens that the pages of this story can be read in any order. Turn the little metal lever, take off the top, and pull out the pages one by one.

DIGESTIVES

In the British Isles a popular snack is a sweet cracker known as a digestive biscuit. It earned its name from the belief that it had antacid properties due to the use of sodium bicarbonate. I don't know whether they really help with digestion, but I do know the biscuits are yummy. This project is a takeoff on the idea of easily digestible information. Laminated pages from an old *Reader's Digest Condensed Book* are cut into cracker shapes and packaged in a repurposed round box. Munch, munch, crunch, crunch—page by page, it goes down smooth.

GATHER

Basic Bookmaking Tool Kit (page 13)

Box or container for your "digestives" (I used a blank paper box from the craft store)

Old *Reader's Digest Condensed Book*

Weights (page 18)

Pinking shears

Shellac brush

Shellac

Milk paint and/or acrylic paint

Paintbrushes

Neutral shoe polish

MAKE

1. Measure your container to determine the "cracker" size you will make, allowing enough room to easily remove the crackers from the box.

2. Tear out the *Reader's Digest* pages and glue one on top of the other until they reach the desired thickness. Each of my crackers is made up of 20 pages. Remember that the edges are cut with pinking shears, so there will be a limit to the thickness that can be cut. Ⓐ

3. Put your glued pages under a weight for 24 hours. It takes a while for the glue in so many layers to fully dry.

4. Cut out the "crackers." I started with a craft knife and metal ruler to cut them down to the approximate size and then used the pinking shears for the exact size. It's much easier to trim the crackers with the shears than to use them to cut the pages down. It takes some muscle to cut through all those layers!

5. Use a needle tool to punch holes in your crackers so that they more closely resemble real crackers.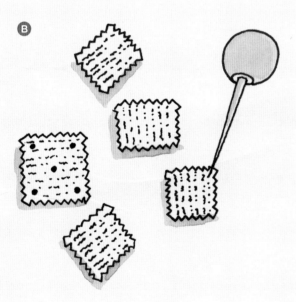

6. Brush the pieces with shellac, being sure to coat the edges and holes. Let dry.

7. Paint the box with milk paint, acrylic paint, or a combination of the two. I used both—milk paint for the overall color and acrylic paint to embellish.

8. Rub the box with natural shoe polish to give it a finished look.

9. Add the "crackers" and enjoy!

B

BOTTLE CAP ACCORDION

Doesn't everyone have a bottle cap collection? No? Well, then, start looking for a couple of caps you can shape into decorative covers! Linen thread runs through the center of the shaped accordion folds, acting as both a practical binder and a decorative element. Add content or leave it blank—either way, it's reminiscent of a toy accordion.

MAKE

1. First, figure out whether you want to preserve the existing painted surface of your bottle caps or paint over it. If you do want to preserve it, cover the outside with a piece of clear packing tape.

2. Flatten the bottle caps with the round-head hammer. I do this by first lightly hammering out the crimped edge with the rounded end of the hammer. Then I use the flat end of the hammer to flatten the whole cap.

3. Remove the rubber disk from the back of each cap. With some caps this can be a bit tricky. Give it a few good blows with the hammer until it starts to break down, then use an awl to dig it out.

4. Hammer the caps again to fully flatten them.

5. Use a dapping block and the rounded edge of the hammer to dome both bottle caps slightly. To create a smooth dome, round each cap a bit at a time. If the cap edges start to fold, flatten the edge and begin again rounding the cap gradually. Before I had a dapping block I used a heavy wooden salad bowl to dome metal (see Shaping Tin on page 42).

6. Using flat-nosed pliers, flatten out the rim of each cap approximately $3/16$ inch (4.5 mm) all the way around, creating a flange.

7. File the underside of the rim (the flange you just made) to rough it up so the glue will have something to grab on to. File the outside edges of the rim to smooth out any sharp edges. Then run sandpaper over the edge.

8. From the inside of each cap, punch a hole in the center with the awl. File the burr from the hole without scraping the outside paint.

9. Remove the tape. Sometimes the tape is hard to remove, so use Goo Gone to help with this process.

10. Wash the caps with dish detergent to remove all oil and dirt. This is important if you are going to paint the caps but also so the glue will bond well with the metal surface. Dry everything well.

11. Paint the caps, if desired.

12. Trace the outside edge of each cap onto thin shirt board or heavy card stock. Cut out the pieces. Double-check the sizing:

GATHER

Basic Bookmaking Tool Kit (page 13)

Thin shirt board or heavy card stock, 3 x 5 inches (7.6 x 12.7 cm)

1 sheet of Rives BFK or other heavy paper, 11 x 14 inches (27.9 x 35.6 cm)

2 bottle caps, similar in size

Clear packing tape (optional)

Round-head hammer

Awl

Dapping block (page 42)

Flat-nosed pliers

Metal file

Sandpaper: 150 grit

Goo Gone (optional)

Liquid dish detergent

Paint and paintbrushes (optional)

Japanese hole punch with 3 mm tip (page 14)

Drawing, painting, and/or collage materials for illustrating the pages (see Creative Techniques, page 28; optional)

Linen thread

Two $1/2$-inch (1.3 cm) 2-hole buttons

Two $1/4$-inch (6 mm) 2-hole buttons

Beacon 527 Multi-Use Glue

Damp rag for wiping up glue

A soft weight (such as a small bag of sand or dried beans)

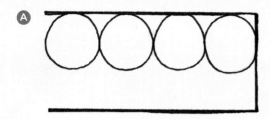

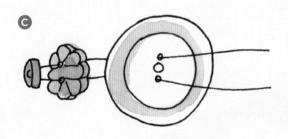

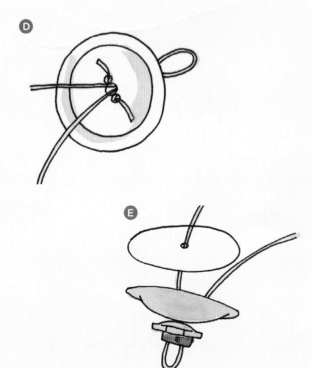

the cutouts should be exactly the same size, or slightly smaller, than the cap.

13. Sand the edges of the shirt board to taper them.

14. Punch a small hole in the center of each board with a Japanese hole punch.

15. Cut a strip of Rives BFK paper: it should be a little wider than the diameter of your cap and 12 inches (30.5 cm) long. Make this piece even longer if you want more than seven folds.

16. Starting at one end of the strip, lightly trace the outline of your board with a pencil. Continue to trace a total of eight circles with the board down the strip, overlapping it just a bit each time. **A** Cut out the whole piece along the outlines.

17. Fold the pages accordion style (page 20), erase the outline tracing lines, and trim the pages to match, if necessary.

18. With the drawing, painting, or collage supplies, decorate and add content to the pages, if desired.

19. Stack all pages and use a needle tool to mark the centers. Punch each page of the accordion with the Japanese hole punch. When you're finished, the center holes should line up.

20. Glue the shirt board to the first and last pages of the accordion using a glue stick.

21. Cut a piece of linen thread the length of your unfolded accordion plus 8 inches (20.3 cm). Guide the linen thread from the inside of one cap out into one hole of a $^1/_2$-inch (1.3 cm) button and then through one hole of a $^1/_4$-inch (6 mm) button. Loop back and go down through the other hole of the $^1/_4$-inch (6 mm) and then the $^1/_2$-inch (1.3 cm) button **B** and finally through the cap again.

22. Tie a double knot at the end (inside the cap) and pull the buttons tight. Trim the tail to $^1/_4$ inch (6 mm).

23. Put a bead of 527 glue on and around the knot. It's good if it seeps through to the buttons so they are set firmly, but don't use so much glue that you see it on the buttons. Let the glue dry completely.

24. Thread the other end of the linen thread through the center hole in the back of the first page of the accordion, and then all the way through the other pages.

25. Separate the cap from the back of the first page. Run a thin bead of 527 glue around the edge of the back of the cap flange. Press the cap and board together. Wipe away any excess glue. Place everything on a flat surface with a soft weight (such as a bag of dried beans or a small sand bag) on top until the glue is set.

26. Cut 5 inches (12.7 cm) of linen thread. Tie a double knot at one end of the thread.

27. Punch two tiny holes on either side of the center hole of the remaining cap. File any burrs.

28. Thread the unknotted end of the short thread up through one of the tiny side holes in the back of the cap, then through the 1/2-inch (1.3 cm) and the 1/4-inch (6 mm) buttons. Loop back through the other holes of the 1/4-inch (6 mm) and the 1/2-inch (1.3 cm) buttons and into the other side hole of the cap, leaving the thread loose. **C**

29. Take the long linen thread from the cap with the accordion attached and thread it up through the middle hole of the back of the second cap. Continue up through the 1/2-inch (1.3 cm) and 1/4-inch (6 mm) buttons. Loop back into the other hole of the 1/4-inch (6 mm) and 1/2-inch (1.3 cm) buttons, then through the middle hole of the cap; the buttons are double threaded.

30. Pull the 5-inch (12.7 cm) length of thread tightly and tie a knot at the base of the second hole. Trim the tails to 1/4 inch (6 mm). **D**

31. Put a bead of 527 glue on both knots, but don't get any glue around the center hole. Let the glue dry completely.

32. Stretch out the accordion so the pages are fully extended and the unglued shirt board is up against the flange of the cap, as it would be if it were glued. Leave a small loop of linen thread extending from the small button on the outside so there will be something to grab on to when you pull the book closed. **E**

33. Maintaining the current length of the linen thread, gently push the pages of the accordion together so it is folded up toward the glued end. You should still have a small loop extending from the small button.

34. Tie a double knot in the linen thread as close to the middle hole of the inside of the cap as possible. Put a bead of 527 glue on the knot and around it without clogging the center hole and restricting the movement of the long thread that winds through the accordion. Let the glue dry completely.

35. Glue the shirt board to the flange of the cap. Wipe off any excess glue.

36. Use the loop to pull the book closed. To open, pull from the edges of each bottle cap.

WHEELIE BIRD

The shaped accordion text block from the Bottle Cap Accordion (page 106) is expanded here to incorporate a shaped cover made from book board. From there, found objects, wire, and buttons are combined to make a nest for the book. This holder enables the book to be displayed upright, but it also creates an environment for the bird and becomes a continuation of the story that's held between the folds of the accordion. The separate elements are both complementary and integral to the overall story.

MAKE

THE BOOK

1. Decide on the shape of your book and the content inside. Using scissors, cut out two covers from the shirt board.

2. File the shirt-board edges with an emery board. Paint the back and front of each cover with acrylic paint.

3. Trace one of your covers onto a piece of card stock and cut it out. This will be a template for your accordion pages.

4. Lightly trace your template onto Rives BFK paper, overlapping the template ⅛ inch (3 mm) on each "page" for the desired number of accordion pages.

5. Cut out the pages using scissors. Ⓐ

6. Fold the pages, erase the tracing lines, and trim the pages to match, if needed.

7. Decorate and add content to the pages with the drawing and collage materials.

8. Glue the first and last pages to the covers with a glue stick. Use the bone folder to remove air bubbles. Put these pieces under a weight with waxed paper between each page and sandwiching each cover.

GATHER

Basic Bookmaking Tool Kit (page 13)

Shirt board, 8 x 10 inches (20.3 x 25.4 cm)

1 sheet of Rives BFK paper, 12 x 4 inches (30.5 x 10.2 cm)

Scrap card stock

Emery board

Acrylic paint and paintbrushes

Drawing or collage materials for illustrating the story (see Creative Techniques, page 28)

Weight (page 18)

Waxed paper

Wire champagne cage

Flat-nosed pliers

Awl

Metal file

Gloves (page 41)

14-ounce (392-g) tin-can lid

Rubber mallet

Bench block (flat piece of steel, at least ¼ inch [6 mm])

Round-head hammer

Dapping block (page 42)

Bottle cap

Fine-point permanent marker

Fine steel wool

Spray paint

Wire cutters

12 inches (30.5 cm) of 14-gauge wire

2 yards (1.8 m) of 24-gauge wire

1 square of felt

Beacon 527 Multi-Use Glue

⅛-inch (3 mm) eyelet (a small grommet)

Eyelet punch

2 beads

Four ¾-inch (1.9 cm) 4-hole buttons

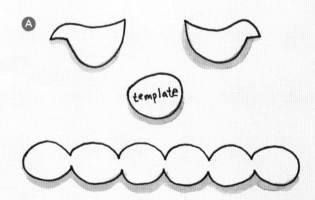

Ⓐ template

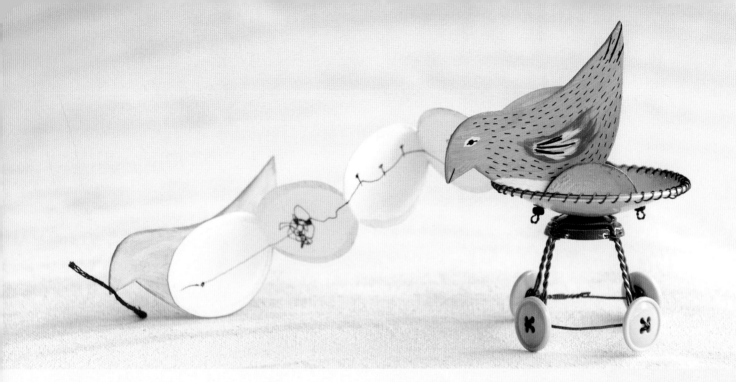

THE STAND

1. Straighten out the lower rim of the wire champagne cage using flat-nosed pliers. Remove the cap from the cage if it hasn't already fallen out.

2. Using the awl, punch a hole in the center of the cage cap to accommodate the ⅛-inch (3 mm) eyelet.

3. Punch tiny holes on either side of the four indentations along the side of the cage cap using the needle tool or awl. File any burrs using a metal file.

4. Wear gloves while handling the tin-can lid. If the lid has indented concentric circles on it, completely flatten the can lid using a rubber mallet on the bench block. File off any ragged edges.

5. Using a round-head hammer and a large wooden dapping block or a heavy wooden salad bowl (see Shaping Tin on page 42), hammer the lid until it's concave. To achieve a smooth surface without any buckling, you must alter the shape just a little at a time.

Start hammering your lid inside the shallowest indentation and gradually increase to the deeper indentations. **Ⓑ**

6. Using the awl, punch a hole in the center of the lid to accommodate the eyelet.

7. Punch tiny holes around the rim of the lid using the needle tool, approximately ⅛ inch (3 mm) apart. Make sure you punch from the inside to the outside.

8. File off burrs from the rim and center hole with a metal file. Sometimes punching holes distorts the shape. Hammer again to adjust the shape, if necessary.

9. Flatten the bottle cap with the round-head hammer. Remove the rubber seal if it's present. File the edges if they're sharp.

10. Using the flat-nosed pliers, hold the flattened bottle cap in the middle of the cap. Push up on either side of the edge of the pliers so that you create two half circles with a flat surface in the middle. The flat surface should be the width of the pliers' nose. **Ⓒ**

B

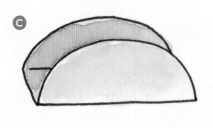

C

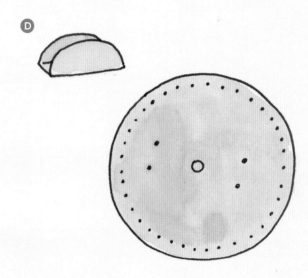

D

11. Place the shaped bottle cap (flat side down) in the center of the shaped tin can lid. It will be sitting above the bottom, resting partway up the lid. With a fine-point permanent marker, mark the two points where the cap rests on the lid.

12. Using the needle tool, punch a hole for each mark (four holes) from the inside out. **D** File any burrs.

13. With your fingers, gently unfold the bottle cap slightly in preparation for painting. It doesn't need to be completely flat again, but just enough so you can paint it easily.

14. Use fine steel wool to prep all surfaces of the tin-can lid, bottle cap, cage, and cage lid. Spray paint these pieces. Be sure to follow safety precautions for spray painting. **E** When the pieces are dry, distress the painted edges with fine steel wool, if desired.

15. Cut a length of 14-gauge wire the circumference of the rim of the tin-can lid. File the ends of the wire so that they overlap smoothly. Gently bend the wire to the shape of the rim using the flat-nosed pliers.

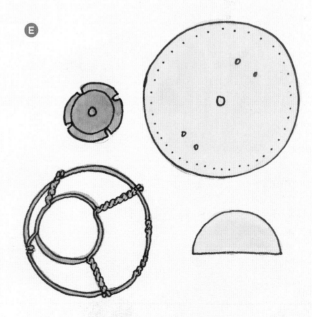

E

16. Cut a length of 24-gauge wire and use it to "sew" the 14-gauge wire to the rim of the can lid with a whipstitch (over and under) through the holes created in step 7. I find it easier to start in the middle and move from side to side rather than sewing from one end to the other. **F**

17. Finish off by wrapping the 24-gauge wire twice at the overlap and ending with both tails on the outside. Twist the ends together. Cut any extra, leaving a ⅛-inch (3 mm) tail. Tuck the tail up under the 14-gauge wire rim.

18. Cut out a round of felt the size of the bottle cap. Glue it to the inside of the cap with 527 glue. Let it dry, and then trim the felt, if necessary.

19. Refold the cap as in step 10.

20. Cut another length of 24-gauge wire and secure the cage cap to the cage using the holes you punched on either side of the indentations on the side of the cap in step 3. **G**

21. Connect the cage to the can lid at their center holes using the eyelet and punch. I do this by placing the whole assembly on a domed surface—like the upturned leg of a wooden stool. Place the parts on the leg, over the eyelet, in this order: eyelet (face down), can lid (face down), and then cage (face down). Punch the eyelet until you have a tight bond.

22. Cut two lengths of 24-gauge wire, approximately 7 inches (17.8 cm) each.

23. Line up the folded bottle cap with the holes inside the tin-can lid.

24. One side at a time, thread one length of wire up through one hole, across the inside of the bottle cap, and down through the other hole. Repeat with the other length of wire on the other side.

25. On the underside of the lid, one side at a time, twist the two ends of the wire together. Trim to ½ inch (1.3 cm). The flat-nosed pliers are helpful in making an even, tight twist. Be careful not to twist too tight or the wire will break off.

26. Thread a bead onto each of the twisted wire ends. Bend the ends of the wire into a circle to create a finished look. **H**

27. "Sew" a button to the bottom of each cage leg with 24-gauge wire, making sure the buttons are tight and stationary.

28. Trim the wire and hide it at the back of the button.

29. Place the book in the bottle cap holder. You can adjust the tightness of the hold by making the fold wider or narrower.

F
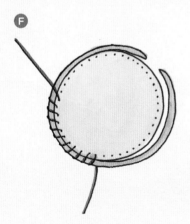

G

H

HEAD CASE

Over the years I have created an ongoing series of functional crowns made from book pages. The source material evokes the original book and a sense of narrative, making an interesting background for the new story on top. These crowns become wearable books, and each one tells a unique story about the wearer.

GATHER

Basic Bookmaking Tool Kit (page 13)

1 yard (91.4 cm) of string

Gloves (page 41)

Wire cutters

8 yards (7.2 m) of binding wire: This can be found at seed and feed stores and some hardware stores; it is also know as bailing wire and is 14- or 16-gauge and oiled to keep it from rusting.

Rag for cleaning binding wire

Flat-nosed pliers

Masking tape

Metal file

1 yard (91.4 cm) of cotton fabric for wrapping headband

Sewing needle with thread to match fabric

30 book pages at least as high as the leaves of your crown

Weights (page 18)

Painting supplies and/or collage materials (see Creative Techniques, page 28)

Japanese hole punch with 1 mm tip (page 14)

Spray fixative (optional)

Shellac or Polycrylic and brush (optional)

Blue painter's tape (optional)

MAKE

1. Use a string to measure the circumference of your head (or the head of the person you're making the crown for). Start in the center of your forehead and go around your head where you want the crown to sit. Cut the string to that length.

2. With gloves on and using wire cutters, cut a length of binding wire approximately 18 feet (5.49 m). The crown frame will be made from one continuous length of wire, which adds stability to the frame because there is no soldering. This long piece of wire is tricky to work with at first, but it becomes easier as you go along.

NOTE: Binding wire is coated with oil to keep it from rusting. This oil is dark and can create a mess. Once I have cut the wire, I use a rag to wipe it several times to remove excess oil. Using gloves helps with manipulating and twisting the wire, as well as protecting your hands from scratches and pokes.

3. Straighten out any kinks or bends in the wire with the flat-nosed pliers. Because the binding wire comes in a coil, the process of uncoiling it often leaves small bends in the wire. You need to smooth these out as best you can.

4. Starting at one end of the length of wire, line up the string from step 1.

5. Put a strip of masking tape on the wire to mark where the string ends.

6. Gently bend the end of the wire to meet the tape mark so you end up with an oval shape. This should match the circumference of your head. Tape the wire together to hold the loop.

7. Continue to wrap the wire around this loop two more times so that you end up with a band of wire made up of three loops. This is the headband of your crown. Use masking tape to hold the bands together. I do this as I go along so I can control the springy wire. Tape well at the point where the third loop ends so that the wire is securely held together and also so that there aren't sharp ends sticking out.

8. At this beginning/ending point of the headband, wrap the remaining wire around the headband two times, keeping the loops that form close together and tight around the headband. These loops around the headband are connector wraps that hold the "leaves" of the crown to the base.

9. Make the first of the crown's leaves by gently bending a large loop away from the headband and then connecting it to the headband with two connector wraps. This will make a leaf about 3 inches (7.6 cm) wide and 7 inches (17.8 cm) high. Repeat this process around the crown, spacing the leaves evenly around the headband. The leaves can be an odd shape if desired, but it is easier not to get too wild with your shapes until you get the hang of the whole construction. **Ⓐ**

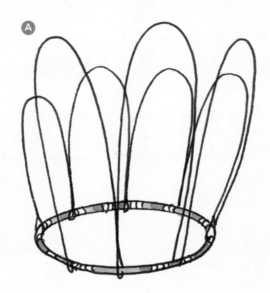

10. Wrap the remaining wire twice more around the headband, intertwining it with the first connector wraps. Cut off any excess wire.

11. File the end of the wire so that it tapers to a dull point and make sure it is snug against the headband so it doesn't stick out.

12. Use the flat-nosed pliers to smooth out the frame where needed.

13. Tear thin strips of cotton fabric approximately ½ inch (1.3 cm) wide and 36 inches (91.4 cm) long. Remove any loose threads.

14. Tape one end of the first strip to the headband next to a connector wrap. Start to evenly wrap the strip around the headband, tightly overlapping the fabric as you go along.

15. Wrap the headband at least three times around with the fabric. This both conceals the taped wire and makes a softer, stronger headband. When you get to the end of one strip, turn the raw edge under ¼ inch (6 mm) and hand-sew it to the next strip. Finish the wrapping close to a connector wrap. Turn the fabric under and hand-sew it to the underside of the headband.

B

a
bee
in
my
bonnet

C

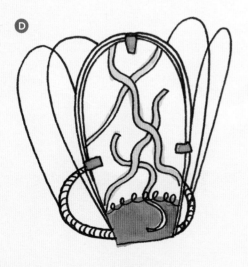

D

16. Glue three book pages together to create heavy paper for each of the leaves of the crown. Put the pages under a weight for four to six hours until completely dry.

17. Lay each leaf frame down on top of a laminated (glued) page. Trace along the inside of the leaf frame. Each leaf will be a different size, so keep track of which leaf goes where and which sides are the front and the back.

18. Cut out the leaves with scissors.

19. Check the fit and trim the leaves if needed. You need to allow approximately $1/16$ inch (1.5 mm) of space all around between the leaf frame and the leaf page.

20. Collage and/or paint the content onto your leaves. Keep in mind that the back of the leaves will be visible, too. **B**

21. Using the Japanese hole punch with the 1 mm tip, punch holes all around the rim of each leaf, approximately $1/8$ inch (3 mm) from the edge of the leaf and $1/8$ inch (3 mm) apart. I generally eyeball this; you can, too. As long as your holes are consistent, they will look even. **C**

22. Gently run the bone folder along the back of the leaf to smooth out any burrs left by the hole punch.

23. Spay both sides of the leaves with fixative, if needed.

24. Sometimes my pages become brittle along the edge. This depends on the quality of the paper. If yours feel brittle, brush the edges of each leaf, front and back, with either shellac (if you want an aged look) or Polycrylic (which will be more invisible).

25. Sew each leaf to its frame with needle and thread. From the front, starting at the bottom left of the leaf frame, sew the leaf to the frame. First sew through the fabric headband and the holes in the leaf. Then, when you turn the corner, sew around the frame and through the holes. End back at the far-left inside corner of the frame. Tie a double knot and hide the knot by pulling it underneath the fabric.

NOTE: As I go along I tape each leaf to its frame with blue painter's tape. This holds the leaf in place while I sew. I only use the smallest amount of tape and only in a few spots. You have to be careful that the tape doesn't remove part of the surface or tear the leaf.

26. Repeat the sewing process in step 25 with each leaf.

TIPS AND NOTES:

— When sewing the leaves to their frames, I generally use a long piece of thread so I don't have to worry about knots as I go along. This can be aggravating and invites trouble, but I do it anyway. If you want to use a shorter thread, tie a square knot (page 24, figure B) to join threads, leaving 1/2-inch (1.3 cm) tails. Once you're done sewing a leaf, go back and put a dab of book glue on the visible knot. Let the glue dry and trim the tails as close to the knot as possible. Be careful here—it's easy to snip threads that you don't mean to!

— As you sew, don't pull the thread too tight or it will rip through the hole. I generally sew most of the leaf and then check to see where the thread needs to be tightened. I gently tighten and ease the thread along until the tension is even all the way around. This keeps any single hole from being under too much stress and prevents tears. If you do strip a hole (it does happen to me!), you can repair it by taking a tiny scrap of the book page and gluing it over the tear. Let the glue dry and start sewing again, being careful not to put stress on that hole until you have sewn further down the line and can distribute the tension evenly.

— You can make a stand to display your crown out of binding wire or purchase one. I usually order one from the Hat Stands and Wig Stands page at www.carefreestore.com.

— The headband can be adjusted to fit your head when you want to wear the crown. Put pressure on the headband very gently to bend it in the desired direction. I have thick, curly hair, which helps hold the crown on my head without it slipping. When I make crowns for other people, I add a round strip of padding around the inside of the headband by sewing a thin tube of fabric (about 1/2 inch [1.3 cm]), turning it inside out to hide the raw edges, and threading cotton upholstery cording through the tube. Then I sew the tube, seam line to the inside, to the inside of the headband, joining the two ends of the tube together with finishing stitches.

STORYBOARD ON WHEELS

Tell a story in a single frame or with interchangeable vignettes. Putting a story on wheels makes it even more fun! This is truly a mixed-media project—tin, wood, paper, and paint all come together to literally build the story. Although my rolling story consists of three "chapters" or panels, the following instructions are for the panel with the house. The same instructions apply for the other panels; just make changes depending on their dimensions. Be sure to read the section on working with tin (page 40) before getting started.

MAKE

NOTE: For this project, it's especially important to wear gloves while working with the tin and wood.

1. Wearing gloves and using tin cutters, cut the tin to your desired shape. Mine is a rectangle approximately 6 x 11 inches (15.2 x 27.9 cm). Because the tin can be difficult to cut precisely, first I cut out a rough shape and then refine it by trimming. File the edges with a metal file to remove any burrs or sharp points.

2. On a flat surface (I use a piece of wooden board), sand the front and back of the tin. Sand it first with the 60-grit, then with the 120-grit sandpaper. It's important to prepare the surface so that there will be a good bond with the paint.

3. Use a green scrubbie and dish detergent to thoroughly clean the tin. Rinse and dry it completely.

4. Paint a base layer of milk paint mixed with Extra Bond on both sides of the tin.

5. Add more layers of milk paint or acrylic paint. Extra Bond isn't needed after the first coat. Let the paint dry overnight.

6. Sand the tin to reveal some of the layers of colors under the top coat. (I have three layers on my panel.) Always use a respirator or dust mask when sanding milk paint.

GATHER

Basic Bookmaking Tool Kit (page 13)

Gloves (page 41)

Tin cutters

Flat tin, 14 x 14 inches (35.6 x 35.6 cm)

Metal file

Sandpaper: 60 and 120 grits

Green scrubbie

Liquid dish detergent

Milk paint

Extra Bond

Paintbrushes

Acrylic paint (optional)

Respirator or dust mask

Painting supplies and/or collage materials (see Creative Techniques, page 28)

Spray fixative

Miter box

Found wood for base of cart, 4 x 11 inches (10.2 x 27.9 cm)

Drill

Drill bits: #64, 1/16 inch (1.5 mm), 1/8 inch (3 mm)

1¾-inch (4.4 cm) hole saw bit

¼-inch (6 mm) birch or oak plywood, 8 x 8 inches (20.3 x 20.3 cm)

Paint or stain for the board, wheels, and axles

Johnson Paste Wax

Marker with smooth barrel, for bending tin (I used a gel pen)

Flat-nosed pliers

Wooden dowels, for the wheel axles, ¼ x 7 inches (6 mm x 17.8 cm); and for panel support, 3/16 x 4 inches (4.5 mm x 10.2 cm)

Eight #2 x ¼ cut tacks

Hammer

Nail set

Wood glue

Spray paint, for thumbtacks

4 thumbtacks

Beacon 527 Multi-Use Glue (optional)

Dovetail saw

Clamp

7. Paint or collage your story on the tin. **A** One thing to keep in mind when creating your image is that there will be two small wooden tabs at the bottom of your tin. These tabs connect to the dowels that support the panel. They will cover a small portion of your image.

NOTE: consider painting a complementary scene or story on the back of the tin so it can be viewed from all angles. I usually do!

8. Spray the side(s) with fixative.

9. Using a miter box, cut the board to the desired size for the cart. Mine is a little shorter than the tin, 4 x 10 inches (10.2 x 25.4 cm).

10. With a drill and a $1^3/_4$-inch (4.4 cm) hole saw bit, cut out four wheels from the $^1/_4$-inch (6 mm) oak or birch plywood. **B**

11. Sand the board and wheels with 60-grit sandpaper, then with 120-grit sandpaper.

12. Paint or stain the board and wheels, if desired. Let dry.

13. Rub the board and wheels with Johnson Paste Wax to give them a protective seal.

14. Cut four small strips of tin measuring $^3/_8$ x $1^1/_2$ inches (1 x 3.8 cm). Cut the edges to round them, and file to remove the burrs.

15. Bend the strips in half over the smooth barrel of a marker to create a U shape. With flat-nosed pliers, turn up the end of each strip $^1/_4$ inch (6 mm).

16. Using a needle tool, punch a hole in each flat, curved end of the strip. Don't bother filing the burrs. **C**

17. Cut two axles for the cart from the $^1/_4$-inch (6 mm) dowel. To find the correct length of the axle, lay the base of the cart face down. Thread two wheels onto the dowel, spacing them so that they straddle the base. Leave $^1/_8$ inch (3 mm) of space between each wheel and the base. **D** Mark the dowel with pencil on the outside

of each wheel. Unthread the wheels. Use a utility knife to cut the dowel at the pencil marks.

18. Drill a hole in the center of each end of the axle using a #64 bit (it's very tiny!).

19. Paint the axles.

20. Nail the tin axle holders to the base of the cart. With the base face down, measure in 1 inch (2.5 cm) from each end. Mark the line with pencil. Center the axle holder over the line $^5/_8$ inch (1.5 cm) in from the side of the cart. Nail it in place. Sometimes I need a nail set to get the nail completely in this tight space. Repeat for all four holders. **E**

21. Put the axles through the holders to make sure they spin freely. Adjust, if needed.

22. Thread the wheels onto the axles (while in the holders) and glue the wheels to the axles with wood glue. The axles and wheels should be flush on the outside. Make sure the wheels are vertical and straight. Let them dry for at least two hours.

23. Spray paint the thumbtacks, if desired. They will be the "hubcaps."

24. Push the thumbtacks into the end holes of the axles to create hubcaps. Glue these in place with 527 glue, if needed. If it's a tight fit, you won't need glue.

25. Make two tabs to hold the storyboard and the supporting dowels. Cut the $^1/_4$-inch (6 mm) plywood into a $^1/_2$ x $^3/_4$-inch (1.3 x 1.9 cm) rectangle. Sand and round the top edges to create a domed shape. **F** The longer the panel, the more dowels you will need to support the panel. If your panel is 8 inches (20.3 cm) or less, one support is enough.

26. Drill a hole $^1/_8$ inch (3 mm) wide in the center of the base of the tab. To do this, mark the position of the hole with a needle tool. Beginning with a $^1/_{16}$-inch (1.5 mm) bit, work your way up to a $^1/_8$-inch (3 mm) bit, drilling approximately $^1/_4$ inch (6 mm) deep at all times.

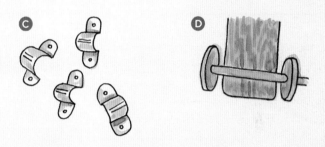

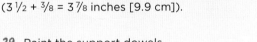

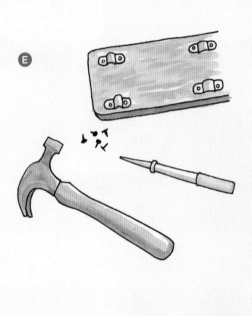

27. Squeezing the tab between your thumb and index finger (with the domed end up), use a dovetail saw to create a slot for the panel to slide into. Gently saw ³⁄₈ inch (1 cm) down from the top. This is a bit tricky; I usually make extra tabs because I often damage or split one here. Squeezing the tab helps avoid splitting.

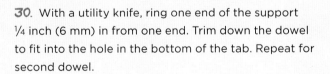

28. Cut the ³⁄₁₆-inch (4.5 mm) dowel for the panel support. Decide how high the panel will sit above the cart (in the one shown, it sits 3 ¹⁄₂ inches [8.9 cm] above). Add ³⁄₈ inch (1 cm) to this measurement, which allows for inserting the tab into the base (3 ¹⁄₂ + ³⁄₈ = 3 ⁷⁄₈ inches [9.9 cm]).

29. Paint the support dowels.

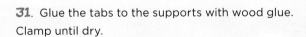

30. With a utility knife, ring one end of the support ¹⁄₄ inch (6 mm) in from one end. Trim down the dowel to fit into the hole in the bottom of the tab. Repeat for second dowel.

31. Glue the tabs to the supports with wood glue. Clamp until dry.

32. Drill two holes in the base for the support dowel using a ¹⁄₈-inch (3 mm) bit.

33. Glue the support dowels to the base with wood glue.

34. Glue the storyboard to the tabs with 527 glue. Pat yourself on the back!

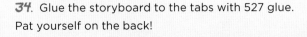

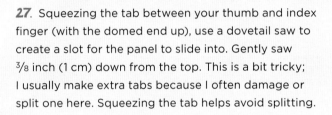

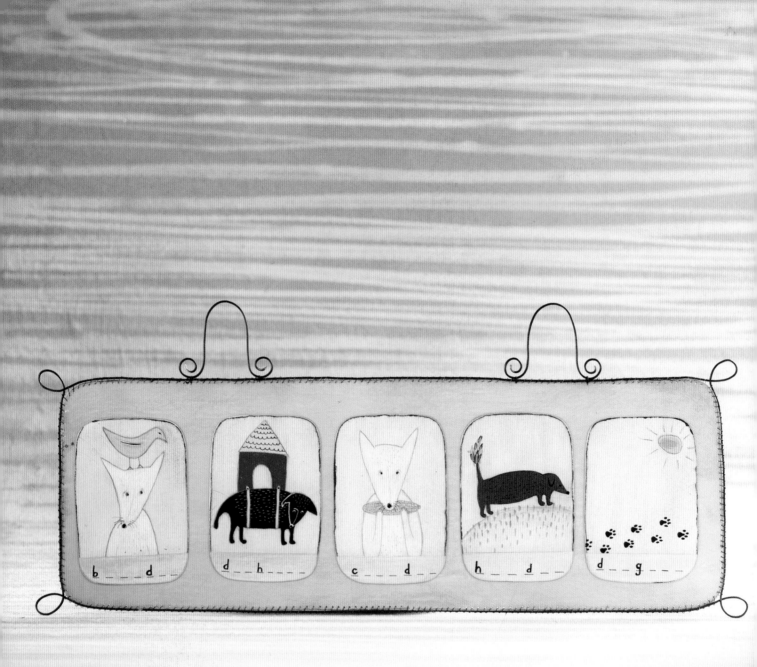

WORD PLAY

This project is a takeoff on kids' board books crossed with fill-in-the blank word puzzles. Images set the stage for the words that must be deciphered. Magnetic sheeting added to the back of the tin "pages" enables the viewer to rearrange the pages at will. Wire sewn around the border adds a decorative finish to the raw edges of the tin and enables the book to be hung on the wall.

MAKE

1. Wearing gloves and using tin cutters, cut one piece of tin 7 x 20 inches (17.8 x 50.8 cm) for the background and five 3 1/2 x 5-inch (8.9 x 12.7 cm) "pages." File the edges to remove burrs and other sharp areas.

2. Sand both sides of the tin first with 60-grit sandpaper, then with 120-grit sandpaper.

3. Wash every piece well with a green scrubbie and dish detergent to make sure the tin is completely clean and grease free. Let them dry.

4. Use milk paint mixed with Extra Bond to coat the tin front and back.

5. Add more layers of milk paint or acrylic paint. (I layered about four colors.) Extra Bond isn't needed after the first coat. Let it all dry completely, preferably overnight.

6. Sand the tin to reveal some of the paint colors underneath the top coat. Always use a dust mask or respirator when sanding milk paint.

7. Collage or paint the pages. First I drew the image lightly with pencil to make sure I could fit the image on the page as well as the text. Next I drew a line across the bottom to separate the text from the image. Then I painted the image and outlined it with pencil. Finally I painted the text area and used a marker to write the letters and dashes.

8. Trace each page onto the magnetic adhesive sheet. Cut them out.

9. Trim the magnetic sheeting 1/8 inch (3 mm) all around so it is slightly smaller than the page you will attach it to.

10. Lightly sand the nonadhesive side of the magnetic sheeting so that the paint will bond. Then paint the nonadhesive side of the magnetic sheeting with acrylic paint.

11. Add images or text to the painted side of the magnetic sheeting, if desired.

GATHER

Basic Bookmaking Tool Kit (page 13)

Gloves (page 41)

Tin cutters

Tin, 14 x 23 inches (35.6 x 58.4 cm)

Metal file

Sandpaper: 60 and 120 grits

Green scrubbie

Liquid dish detergent

Milk paint

Extra Bond (if you're using milk paint)

Paintbrushes

Acrylic paint (optional)

Respirator or dust mask

Painting supplies and/or collage materials (see Creative Techniques, page 28)

Black artist's pen

Magnetic adhesive sheet (found at craft stores), 11 x 14 inches (27.9 x 35.6 cm)

Wire cutters

3 yards (2.7 m) of binding wire: This can be found at seed and feed stores and some hardware stores; it is also known as bailing wire and is 14- or 16-gauge and oiled to keep it from rusting.

Rag for cleaning binding wire

Flat-nosed pliers

Blue painter's tape

6 yards (5.4 m) of 24-gauge wire

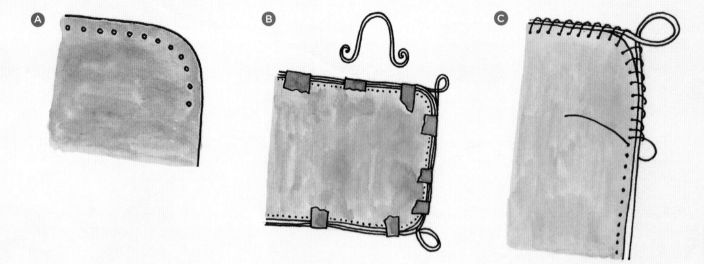

12. Adhere the magnetic sheeting to the back of each page.

13. Using a needle tool, punch small holes along the edge of the background tin. Punch from the front so the burrs are on the back. **Ⓐ** File the burrs.

14. Cut a length of binding wire to use as a border for the background tin. Overestimate what you will need so you have enough. I cut a 2 1/2-yard (2.3 m) length. Bend

it around the background. Add loops, if desired (like the one shown). Flat-nosed pliers can help to smooth out bumpy spots. Use blue painter's tape to hold the wire in place as you work.

NOTE: Binding wire is coated with oil to keep it from rusting. This oil is dark and can create a mess. Once I have cut the wire, I use a rag to wipe it several times to remove excess oil. Using gloves helps with manipulating and twisting the wire, as well as protecting your hands from scratches and pokes.

15. File the two ends of the wire where they meet. The ends should taper so that they overlap and don't stick out. You don't want anything sharp around the edge.

16. Make hangers for the book from binding wire. I took a 6- to 7- inch (15.2 to 17.8 cm) piece of wire and made a loop with spirals on each end. **Ⓑ** File the ends of the wire to taper as you did in step 15.

17. Sew the wire border to the background using 24-gauge wire and a whipstitch (just go over and then under). **Ⓒ** Loose ends of wire can be twisted onto the back, cut to 1/4 inch (6 mm), and tucked up against the border.

18. Sew the hangers to the border with 24-gauge wire. I positioned the hangers 5 inches (12.7 cm) in on both sides. Again, loose ends of wire can be twisted onto the back, cut to 1/4 inch (6 mm), and tucked up against the border.

Describe your installation. Enchanted Beanstalk is an adhesive vinyl mural applied to eight floors of windows on the Children's Hospital in Ann Arbor, Michigan. The design incorporates hundreds of fanciful elements suggesting plant, animal, insect, and human forms; landscapes; architectural environments; and quirky mechanical contrivances in strong colors and varying scales. The designs are applied to the interior of the windows and configured so that when visible from outside they form an intricately woven tapestry, threaded between levels by a climbing vine and other rhythmically sequenced elements. The vine evokes Jack and the Beanstalk, who clambered up into magical worlds, defeated the wicked giant, and brought back the goose that laid the golden egg.

How is this piece a book? The mural is a complex narrative structure. Each floor has a different visual theme and a unique composition, unfolding sequentially along a single, publicly accessible corridor looking out over the city. From inside the building, the viewer can experience only one portion of the design at a time. Everything is designed to create movement, to belong in a specific architectural space while leading to the next one. Like a book, the experience is cumulative, relying on a viewer's capacity to carry memories and impressions from one experience to the next, building a history that ultimately resides in the imagination.

How did this piece grow out of earlier work? My work returns to grids and sequences of images where one is invited to make sense by creating narrative connections across an array of visual units. This mode of thinking has been nurtured in me by a culture of books, but I am astounded also by its emergence in other contexts: Japanese folding screens and European multipanel altar pieces, Giotto's frescoes, and carved narrative reliefs on the walls of ancient sacred sites all over the world. These are all devices for conveying the fourth dimension of time along a visual plane, and they speak to how we as humans make sense of the world through accumulated insights.

What inspires you? Dawn, dusk, and starlight are magical for me. In the half-light, my perceptions go on full alert. I struggle to make sense of partially perceived forms, silhouettes, muted contrasts, distorted spaces, unexpected glimmers. If there is a time of day that prompted the emergence of the human imagination, it was certainly not the clarity of high noon, but more likely the dimly comprehended lusciousness of half-light tangled in shadows. For me, the unexplained is always the most compelling.

I'm inspired by the mystery of who we are, we human beings—how we acquire information through our senses, and from each other, and then what we do with what we get. The world is never quite what we think it is, but somehow we manage. We look at flat, unmoving images and construct spaces and narratives. How does that happen? I am fascinated by sequence, pattern, rhythm, and repetition—in other words, the various structures that make meaning possible. I am curious about where meaning comes from, and suspicious of what we throw away—what we ignore—in our desperate need to comprehend the significance of objects and experiences.

Enchanted Beanstock, Jim Cogswell
PHOTOGRAPH BY JAMES ROTZ

PENCIL BIRDS

What can you do with an old paperback? How can you make the existing story transform into words of flight? Upcycle, repurpose, and recycle all apply here. Cut the book apart, turn it back on itself, add a few structural elements that support the theme, and voilà! You now have a flock of book birds.

MAKE

NOTE: These instructions are for a medium-size bird. Once you get the hang of the process, you can change the dimensions of the book spine for smaller or larger birds.

1. With the book closed, measure down 3 inches (7.6 cm) from the top of the book. With a ruler, draw a line from this measurement across the book.

2. Cut the book all the way through at the line using a guillotine. (You can save the leftover portion of the book to make another bird, if desired.)

3. With a ruler, draw a diagonal line from the top of the spine down to the bottom of your cut book to make a skinny triangle. The wider the triangle, the wider the bird's wingspan.

4. Cut along the line using the guillotine.

5. Holding the cover and the first two pages, open the book and flex the spine to train it to open and wrap evenly around the barrel of the pencil. Repeat this a couple of times.

6. Pull off the cover and any of the first pages that aren't glued securely to the spine.

7. Gather the first 6 to 10 pages on each end. **B** Holding these in your hand, wrap the spine around the barrel of the pencil with the flat of the triangle in the direction of the eraser. Position the spine about 1 inch (2.5 cm) from the end of the eraser. Using a pencil, mark where the

GATHER

Basic Bookmaking Tool Kit (page 13)

Paperback book with a spine at least 1 inch (2.5 cm) in width: The pages still need to be firmly glued without any breaks in the spine. You can tell the book is good for this project if you flip through it quickly and it flows easily without gaps.

Guillotine

Long pencil, new or used

Pencil sharpener

Red ink, marker, or acrylic paint

Sandpaper: 60 grit

Wood glue

2 bulldog clips: #2 for a 3- to 4-inch (7.6 to 10.2 cm) medium-size bird, #1 for a smaller bird, or #4 for a larger bird

Damp cloth for wiping off glue

Note: This project requires a guillotine—don't worry, not that guillotine! The machine you need cuts large stacks of paper at a time. Many book-arts, letterpress, and print studios have one that you can use. Another source is a commercial printer or copy shop. If you draw the outline of the cuts you want, they may be willing to cut the book for you.

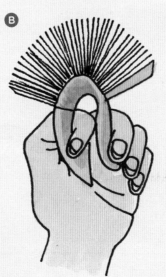

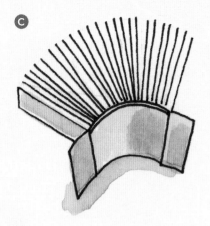

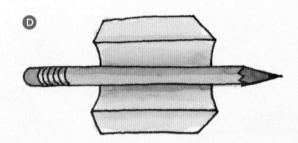

other end of the spine meets the pencil barrel. From this point, measure up 1½ inches (3.8 cm) on the pencil. This last mark will be the tip of the pencil once it is sharpened.

8. Sharpen the pencil.

9. Color the exposed wood at the sharpened end of the pencil with red ink, marker, or acrylic paint.

10. Sand along the portion of the pencil barrel that will be covered by the book so that the glue will bond well.

11. With scissors, cut each end of the 6 to 10 pages straight across ½ inch (1.3 cm) from the spine. These will be trimmed up later, so don't worry if they aren't completely even.

12. Glue the cut pages together (but not to the rest of the book) using a glue stick to create a flange. **C**

13. Brush wood glue along the spine and flanges of the book.

14. Wrap the book around the pencil. The flanges should meet and glue together. **D**

15. Clamp the flanges tight together using two bulldog clips. Clean up any oozing glue with a damp rag. Let everything dry completely, about three to four hours.

16. When it's dry, remove both bulldog clips.

17. Trim the flange to even it up.

18. Center one bulldog clip on the flange. Now your bird has legs!

19. Paint red rings around the pencil for decoration, if desired.

Describe "creative journaling." Creative journaling is an integral part of my creative process. I have used sketchbooks and journals in varying degrees all my life. My muses come from the environment surrounding me and the continually evolving inner world of the subconscious. This outer world is filtered through a series of ongoing creative journals. Creating with my hands allows me to process and transform my experiences and responses into different forms of art. Between the experiencing and the translation of this essence into the art that they inspire there is a convoluted distillation process that takes place between the covers of my journals. In various different journals I record and filter the world around me, basically my way of making sense of life.

Why is journaling important to your creative process?
As an artist I explore a theme in my work for an extended period of time, a decade or more. The idea of a journey has been a constant in my work for more than 20 years, though the work has shifted from architecturally inspired imagery to vessel or boat motifs. Similarly, my medium has evolved from textiles to include mixed media. My journals have inspired and recorded these shifts. When I am captivated by something, it undergoes its initial distillation when it is translated into my vocabulary and recorded in my journals. I generally do not simply record what has captivated me. The act of recording an image, words, ideas, and events helps imprint it in my subconscious. I reread my journal, but the important act of recording, of redrawing a pencil sketch, of filling in with color and tone all help to acquaint and reacquaint myself with what inspired me at that moment. It is an investment in my relationship with my creative intuition. I have a shoulder bag/purse that was purchased to fit the journal that I always have with me. This book, what I call my annual journal, is kept in this purse except when in use, so that it is always ready to go with me. My entries are a combination of images and free-verse word poems of sorts. This journal is one of many that support and channel my creative ideas, so that when I am in the studio working I am never at a loss. The creative journals keep my creativity primed and ready.

My journals are an anchor of sorts, harbingers for the future directions in my work as well as an archive of ideas and events past. They forecast where my work is headed, yet I can only see these threads of continuity after the fact. I trust in my creative process, my creative journey, and my journals are a fellow traveler on this path. They reflect what I respond to, distilling out what has affected me. By the nature of the book form itself, the ideas are kept in order, neat, compact, and accessible. In the beginning my journals were purchased; more and more I create specific journals for specific purposes.

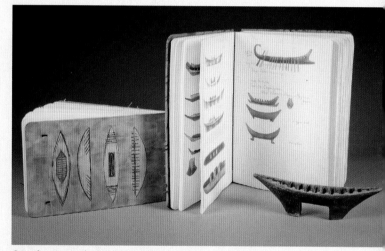

Creative Journals and 3D Maquette, Heather Allen-Hietala
PHOTOGRAPH BY NICK LAFONE

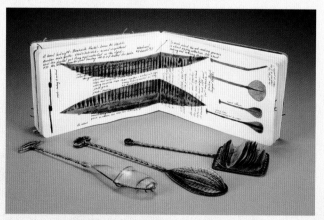

Hawaii Journal and Inspired Instruments of Motion,
Heather Allen-Hietala
PHOTOGRAPH BY NICK LAFONE

THE DISPENSER

Much like a book dispensing its story, this project unspools a story one sentence at a time. One roll of tape can be considered a book. It's up to you whether that book contains single-sentence short stories or sayings to keep your life on track. I used my trusty manual typewriter to write my "books," but handwritten or computer-printed text works, too. You could even use text from a deconstructed book!

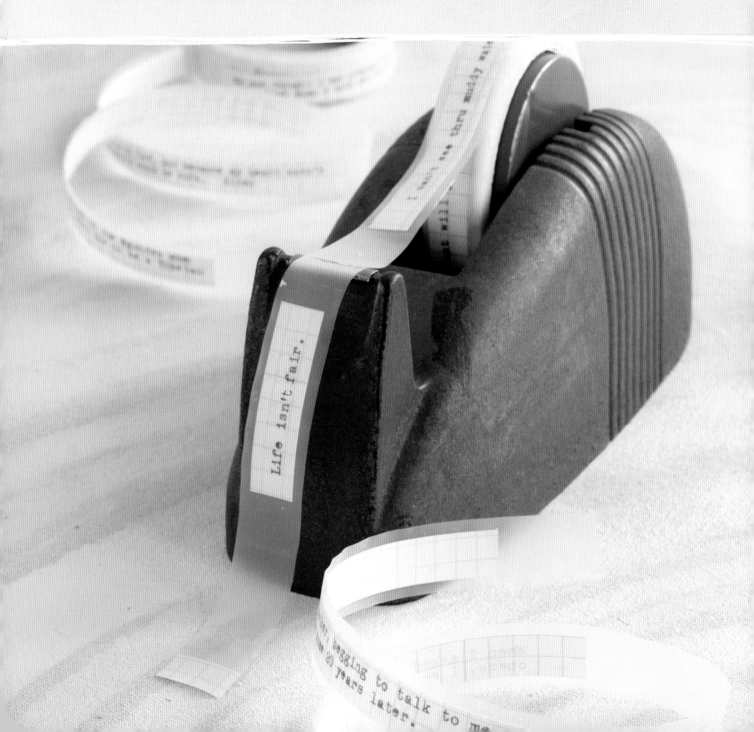

MAKE

1. Start by writing or printing your story (or sayings) on paper. Cut the story into strips about ½ inch (1.3 cm) wide.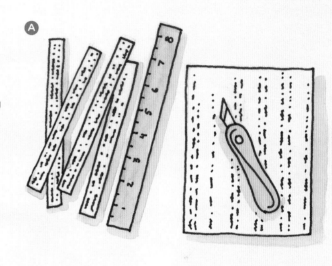

2. With its sticky side up, unwind a length of invisible tape across a long table. Take a separate piece of tape and secure the beginning of the length of tape to the table so it won't move. Let the spool hang over the other end of the table so that the tape is taut with the sticky side is up.

NOTE: You will only be working on a portion of the tape at first, not the whole roll.

3. If your story has a beginning and an ending, arrange the paper strips in a backward order; you will tape the end of the story down first, working back to the beginning. Starting several inches (cm) from the end of the tape, center the paper strips and press them gently so they stick to the tape. The words of your story should be face down against the sticky side of the tape. Space your strips ½ to 2 inches (1.3 to 5.1 cm) apart. B

4. Wind the tape onto an empty spool, being sure to keep it even on the sides.

5. Repeat steps 2–4 until all the strips are applied and wound onto the spool. Don't work all the way to the end of the tape, though—you need to leave a little bit of tape to pull before the story starts! I added a small tab of paper at the end (which is the beginning of the story!) so there is something to grab—the same way a new roll of tape has a tab to pull when starting a roll. C

6. Place the spool in the tape dispenser and let the story begin!

When I found this old metal tape dispenser at a junk store, I imagined it must have a story to tell. But you don't need a vintage tape dispenser to make this project—any one will do. The only difference will be the size of the spool. You can either recycle empty spools or make ones from a dowel.

GATHER

Basic Bookmaking Tool Kit (page 13)

A printed story, sayings, fortunes, or other text for the book

Full roll of ¾-inch (1.9 cm) invisible tape

1 or 2 empty tape spools

Tape dispenser

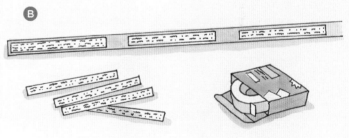

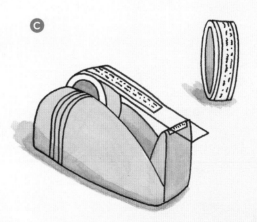

AIR MAIL

Papier-mâché is so versatile! It works well in combination with all types of materials. Here I combine it with an old receipt spindle, but I've also combined papier-mâché birds on top of crowns, and papier-mâché dogs with casters as roller skates. For several years now I've made a whole series of papier-mâché birds and dogs with books in their mouths. This bird is a prime example.

MAKE

THE BIRD

1. Crumple up newspaper to create the shape of a bird. My bird is about 3 inches (7.6 cm) wide and 10 inches (25.4 cm) long. I used five full sheets of newspaper to form the body and another half sheet for the head. Use masking tape to hold the shape together. Ⓐ

2. Tear strips of newspaper. You'll need quite a bit ready for the next step, so tear up about four full sheets.

3. Lay down a length of aluminum foil as a work surface. Foil is good because the wallpaper paste won't stick to it. Coat the bird with wallpaper paste. Coat strips of newspaper one at a time with the wallpaper paste and wrap the bird. Keep the strips smooth—you don't want any folds or buckles. Layer strips three or four times going in different directions all over the bird. Let it dry.

4. Repeat step 3. When the bird dries this time, it should be hard and not flexible at all. If it is still flexible, repeat step 3 again until the outside shell of the bird is hard. Ⓑ

5. Mark the bird's beak with a pencil where the slit for the book will be. Using a craft knife, cut along the mark. Several cuts will be needed to create a wide enough opening. If the slit gets too ragged, use PVA to glue the ragged areas into place.

GATHER

Basic Bookmaking Tool Kit (page 13)

Lightweight or decorative text paper

Newspaper, 16 to 20 sheets

Masking tape

Aluminum foil

Wallpaper paste, 2 cups (500 g)

Brush for applying wallpaper paste

PVA glue

Awl

Acrylic paints

Milk paint (optional)

Paintbrushes

Found-object stand: I used an old restaurant receipt spindle, but you can use a dowel on a block of wood or a small lamp base.

Wood glue if stand is wood or Beacon 527 Multi-Use Glue if stand is metal

Canceled stamps

Thread or 1-ply linen thread

Sewing needle

Note: For single-ply linen thread, untwist a short length of 3- or 4-ply linen thread and separate the individual plies or strands.

Ⓐ

Ⓑ

6. Use PVA on the edge of a fettling knife to get glue inside the beak. Try your best to smooth out the inside and create a flat, rigid surface. Once the glue is dry, repeat this process if necessary.

7. Mark the spot on the bird's belly where the stand will be attached and use an awl to punch a hole there. Do this gently so that the bird's belly isn't torn or crushed as you push in the awl.

8. Paint the bird. If I want some of the newspaper text to show through, I start with watered-down liquid acrylics as a wash and follow with full-strength paint for details and decorative elements. If I don't care about the text, I use full-strength milk paint or acrylics. It's hard to tell it's a bird until I paint on defining features like wings and eyes. They really bring it to life!

9. Paint the stand with milk paint, if desired.

10. Glue the bird to the stand with wood glue or 527 glue if the stand is metal. Let dry completely.

THE BOOK

NOTE: My book is a single signature measuring 1½ x 2 inches (3.8 x 5.1 cm). I didn't use any cover paper, just text paper so the book would be skinny and fit into the bird's beak.

1. Cut or tear lightweight paper for the signature (page 23). The book shown is eight pages (two sheets). For content, I glued in canceled stamps that related to the bird.

2. Bind the book with a three-hole pamphlet stitch (page 24) using thread or 1-ply linen thread. Because my book is so small I didn't make a template for the sewing stations. Once I had my two sheets folded in half for my signature, I simply used my sewing needle to punch three evenly spaced holes for the sewing stations. Because it is such a tiny book, you can eyeball where the holes should be.

3. Insert the book so that the bird holds it in its beak.

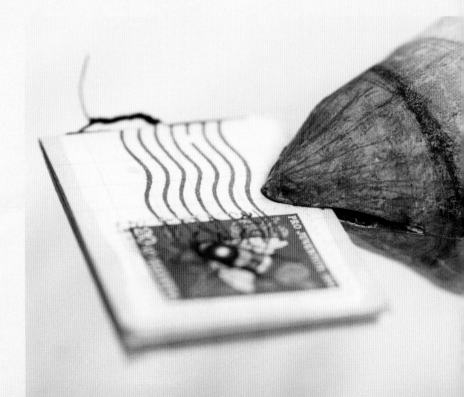

BOOK BALL

This project was inspired by Dolph Smith's *Roll Your Own: A Journal of Random Thoughts* (see page 141). It's essentially a "self-printing" book: the book is reimagined as a collection of words that can be combined with physical action, random chance, and a sense of adventure to tell a different story every time. Go ahead, roll the ball and let the story unfold.

GATHER

Basic Bookmaking Tool Kit
(page 13)

Newspaper, 16 to 20 full sheets

Wallpaper paste, 2 cups (500 g)

Brush for wallpaper paste

Rubber ball, 6 inches (15.2 cm) in
diameter (I used a cheap kid's rubber
ball from the drugstore)

Acrylic paints

Paintbrushes

Words for your story (cut from
a book, typed, or printed from
the computer)

MAKE

1. Tear strips of newspaper. Coat them in wallpaper paste and layer the strips on the rubber ball. Let them dry completely.

2. Repeat this layering process three times, or until the ball feels hard to the touch when it's dry.

3. Using a pencil, draw 1-inch (2.5 cm) squares around the outside "equator" of the ball, leaving at least 1 inch (2.5 cm) between the squares.

4. Cut out the squares with a craft knife. This will puncture the rubber ball right off the bat. Be careful while you are cutting out the squares. You don't want to cut yourself or push so hard on the papier-mâché ball that it collapses. Make sure the blade in your knife is sharp and go slowly so you have more control. **A**

5. Remove the deflated ball. To do this, put the cutting edges of a pair of scissors through a square and snip at the rubber until it's in pieces. **B** Then pull the pieces out through the open squares.

6. Coat the inside of the papier-mâché ball with wallpaper paste to secure any loose strips. Let it dry.

7. Add more newspaper strips coated in paste to the outside of the ball and along the raw edges of the cut squares. Let them dry.

8. Repeat step 7 until the ball is hard and really feels solid.

9. Paint the inside of the ball with acrylics first, and after that has dried move to the outside. The ball wants to roll around, so you might have to paint it in stages. For the outside I painted a wash of color (watered-down acrylic) to retain some of the text. Next I followed with undiluted paint in patterns. Finally I came in with a pencil to outline the circles.

10. For the words of the story, I took a segment of my written text for this book, enlarged the words, and then printed them out. You can use almost any random collection of sentences, and it will work just as well.

11. Cut the words apart. **C**

12. Fill the ball with the words and roll it! **D**

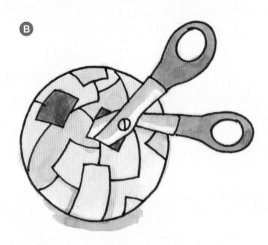

(B)

(C)

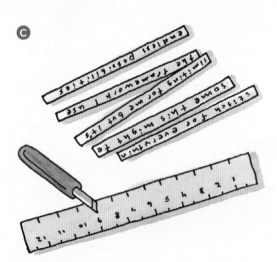

(D)

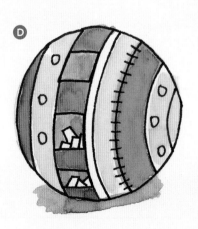

ARTIST FEATURE DOLPH SMITH

Why do you make books? A Princeton physicist was once asked why on earth he was doing a study of the aerodynamics of paper airplanes. His answer: "If we knew what we were going to discover, it just wouldn't be research, would it?" Were I to paraphrase, I might reply, "If we knew what we were going to make, it just wouldn't be a creative act, would it?" So I make books because wI am curious. One might argue that a painting reveals itself instantly. You take it in over time, but it is presented as a visual whole, whereas a book reveals itself slowly over time. A book leads one along a pathway, at each stage a new revelation.

A book is built the same way. I begin with a notion. Notion becomes motion. The book becomes a kinetic happening. A path forms. Why not a 3-D illustration in this 3-D object? Wooden covers? With windows? Sweet mystery. Put books on stilts? That is why I make books. They are not goal oriented but rather path oriented. Like the path Robert Frost took. He started on a journey and found choices. I like that. I let my curiosity lead me to a path, and then I celebrate the choices I find there. Hopefully, like Frost, I take the one that makes all the difference.

Describe your approach to materials and tools.
Tools and materials can be seductive. I have a table saw, a scroll saw, a band saw, and lots of wood blanks and pieces. I have to be carefully determined to make a book and not a coffee table for it to go on. Don't be tool foolish. They are there to facilitate an idea and not to tell one what to do. However, I do love woods. It is unrequited love, because I have no idea about wood properties or how to use it. I just see potential. I have found that I am a wood hoarder. I grab odd pieces at a lumberyard, bring them to the studio, and watch them for days, weeks. Then I see something in a piece and the journey begins.

What inspires you? Storytelling. I try to give my books a strong narrative component. A search for the visual story. My first books were "picture" books. The words came later. Comic books?! Those little individual cells with all that pictorial action. Humor . . . the visual pun.

Do you think of yourself as a book artist? Yes, but my history began in an ad agency fifty years ago. I trained in advertising design. That was a good thing, because design is at the heart of all we do as artists, regardless of our label. But advertising at that time was unfulfilling. Even boring! So I began, as Frost did, to seek the road less traveled. I found watercolor. I discovered it to be an act of nature. Mother Nature has a way of finishing a watercolor painting. She causes watermarks, celebrates the way one pigment blends with another. Pigments do come from natural sources, and one will stain and another will be gritty and settle into the interstices of the paper. I like that.

Then I learned to make handmade paper. I thought it would make me a better painter. It didn't. It led to even more diverse ways of expression. Making one's own substrate is pretty nifty. Another act of nature in the drying process. But that led finally to books. One makes paper, one makes books. So, back to the question. No, I do not think of myself as a book artist. Because I use all of the above I assume the label of "a body of workist"! Still, all I can think about when I go into my studio is starting a new book!

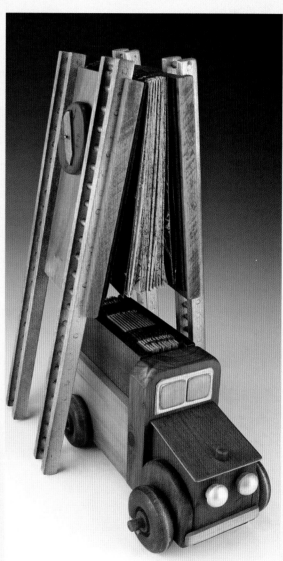

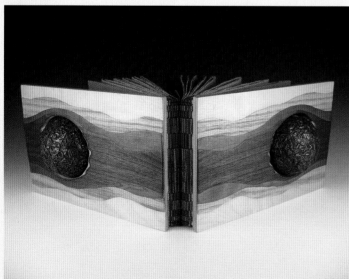

Clockwise from top left:

Roll Your Own: A Journal of Random Thoughts, Dolph Smith
PHOTOGRAPH BY DOLPH SMITH

Need a Lift, Dolph Smith
PHOTOGRAPH BY DOLPH SMITH

Buoyk, Dolph Smith
PHOTOGRAPH BY DOLPH SMITH

RESOURCES

This list only includes suppliers I use or refer to in the book, but there are many other good sources for bookbinding and art and craft supplies out there—from local to large chains. I suggest going online to find the closest supplier in your area, because buying local is a good way to go whenever possible.

PAPER

ARTPAPER.COM
Online retailer
Asheville, NC
www.artpaper.com

DICK BLICK
Storefront in many large cities and online retailer
Galesburg, IL
www.dickblick.com

PAPER SOURCE
Storefront in many large cities and online retailer
Chicago, IL
www.paper-source.com

REX ART
Storefront and online retailer
Miami, FL
www.rexart.com

BOOKBINDING SUPPLIES

HOLLANDER'S
Storefront and online retailer
Ann Arbor, MI
www.hollanders.com

TALAS
Storefront and online retailer
Brooklyn, NY
www.talasonline.com

LINEN THREAD

ROYALWOOD, LTD.
Storefront and online retailer
Mansfield, OH
www.royalwoodltd.com

MILK PAINT

THE OLD FASHIONED MILK PAINT CO., INC.
Online retailer
Groton, MA
www.milkpaint.com

TOOLS

HIGHWATER CLAYS
Storefront and online retailer
Asheville, NC
www.highwaterclays.com

MICRO-MARK
Online retailer
Berkeley Heights, NJ
www.micromark.com

RIO GRANDE
Online retailer
Albuquerque, NM
www.riogrande.com

REFERENCE BOOKS

Diehn, Gwen. *Real Life Journals: Designing & Using Handmade Books*. Asheville, NC: Lark Books, 2010.

Golden, Alisa. *Making Handmade Books: 100+ Bindings, Structures & Forms*. Asheville, NC: Lark Books, 2011.

Hansson, Bobby. *The Fine Art of the Tin Can: Techniques & Inspirations*. Asheville, NC: Lark Books, 2005.

LaPlantz, Shereen. *Cover to Cover: Creative Techniques for Making Beautiful Books, Journals & Albums*. Asheville, NC: Lark Books, 1998.

Meyer, Helga. *The Contemporary Craft of Paper Mache*. Asheville, NC: Lark Books, 1996.

New, Jennifer. *Drawing from Life: The Journal as Art*. New York: Princeton Architectural Press, 2005.

Smith, Keith A. *Books without Paste or Glue*. Vol. 1 of Non-Adhesive Binding. 3rd rev. ed. Rochester, NY: Sigma Foundation, 1999.

ACKNOWLEDGMENTS

This book is dedicated to Dan, who always sees the best in me.

Grateful appreciation to my community of fellow book people here in Asheville and especially to those in my critique group: Lisa Blackburn, Frank Brannon, Clara Boza, Laurie Corral, Gwen Diehn, Michelle Francis, Heather Hietala, and Laura Ladendorf. I am fortunate to be surrounded by thoughtful, generous people living creative lives.

An additional thanks to Laurie Corral of BookWorks for making her dream of a creative community centered around books, paper, print (and more!) come true for the benefit of all.

Double thanks to Gwen Diehn for her help and feedback in the planning stages of this book. Her vast experience and willingness to share her knowledge made the mysteries of writing a how-to book a little clearer and a lot less scary.

Much obliged and a basketful of dark chocolate to Dolph, Doug, Gwen, Frank, Heather, and Jim for rounding out this book in ways I never could.

A special thanks to all the folks at Lark who made this possible: Nicole McConville for pitching the idea and going to bat for it; Thom O'Hearn, my editor, who came into the book midstream and grabbed the bull by the horns; Kristi Pfeffer, art director extraordinaire; Lynne Harty for the beautiful photographs; Sue Havens for the equally beautiful Illustrations; and Kathleen McCafferty, also my editor—who could have a better cheerleader than you?

Eternal gratitude to Penland School of Crafts for asking me to be a part of their community for three years. I wish everyone had the same gift of time to explore their passion.

And finally to my parents, Kitty and Coochy Couch, who instilled in me an appreciation for handmade objects and kindness toward others.

ABOUT THE AUTHOR

Margaret Couch Cogswell is a storyteller with a love of bookmaking. Using simple materials and a low-tech approach, she creates works that speak of her interests and appreciation of the rough, unpolished moments in our lives. She received a BA from Rhodes College and has attended Rhode Island School of Design, Arrowmont School of Arts and Crafts, and Penland School of Crafts, where she was a resident artist from 2008 to 2011. Margaret lives in Asheville, North Carolina, with her husband, Dan, and their two children, Will and Camille.

INDEX

Accordion fold, 20
Acrylic ink, 32
Anatomy of a book, 15

Basic bookmaking tool kit, 13
Binding, 23
Book board, 17
Book cloth, 17
Book cover, 22
Book glues, 19
Bookbinding needles, 16

Collage, 33
Coptic stitch, 26
Corner rounder, 14
Cutting paper and book board, 21
Cutting tin, 42

Deconstructing a can, 41
Dolph Smith, 140
Doug Beube, 70
Drawing, 28

End caps, 17
End sheets, 18

Fabriano paper, 12
Fettling knife, 14
Five-hole pamphlet stitch, 24
Folding paper, 20
Frank Brannon, 84
Fusible interfacing, 35

Gesso, 31
Gloves, 41
Gouache, 31
Gwen Diehn, 54

Hahnmühle Ingres paper, 12
Heather Allen-Hietala, 131

Japanese hole punch, 14
Japanese stab binding, 25
Jim Cogswell, 127
Journaling, 28

Liquid acrylic paint, 31

Making a book cover, 22
Margaret Cogswell, 143
Milk paint, 31
Murano paper, 12

Painting, 31
Painting tin, 42
Paper, 12
Papier-mâché, 38
Papier-mâché recipes, 39

Resources, 143

Safety, 13
Seven-hole pamphlet stitch, 24
Sewing, 35
Shaping tin, 42
Shellac, 32
Signatures, 23
Single needle Coptic stitch, 26

Tearing fabric, 36
Template, 23
Three-hole pamphlet stitch, 24
Tin, 40
Tortillon, 33

Weights, 18
Wire, 43

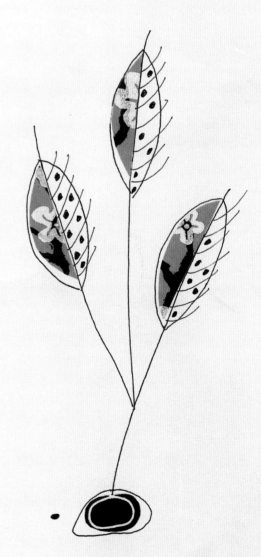